Communication that Counts

LANGUAGE AT WORK

Series Editors: **Jo Angouri**, *University of Warwick, UK* and **Rebecca Piekkari**, *Aalto University Business School, Finland*

Language at Work is a new series designed to bring together scholars interested in workplace research. The modern workplace has changed significantly in recent years. The international nature of business activities and the increasing rate of mobility around the world create a new challenging environment for individuals and organisations alike. The advancements in technology have reshaped the ways employees collaborate at the interface of linguistic, national and professional borders. The complex linguistic landscape also results in new challenges for health care systems and legal settings. This and other phenomena around the world of work have attracted significant interest; it is still common however for relevant research to remain within clear disciplinary and methodological boundaries.

The series aims to create space for exchange of ideas and dialogue and seeks to explore issues related to power, leadership, politics, teamwork, culture, ideology, identity, decision making and motivation across a diverse range of contexts, including corporate, health care and institutional settings. *Language at Work* welcomes mixed methods research and it will be of interest to researchers in linguistics, international management, organisation studies, sociology, medical sociology and decision sciences.

All books in this series are externally peer-reviewed.

Full details of all the books in this series and of all our other publications can be found on http://www.multilingual-matters.com, or by writing to Multilingual Matters, St Nicholas House, 31–34 High Street, Bristol, BS1 2AW, UK.

LANGUAGE AT WORK: 8

Communication that Counts

Language Practice and Ideology in Globalized Accounting

Pia Patricia P. Tenedero

MULTILINGUAL MATTERS
Bristol • Jackson

DOI https://doi.org/10.21832/TENEDE6475
Library of Congress Cataloging in Publication Data
A catalog record for this book is available from the Library of Congress.
Names: Tenedero, Pia Patricia P., author.
Title: Communication that Counts: Language Practice and Ideology in Globalized Accounting/Pia Patricia P. Tenedero.
Description: Bristol, UK; Jackson, TN: Multilingual Matters, [2023] | Series: Language at Work 8 | Includes bibliographical references and index. | Summary: "This book examines language and communication practices and ideologies in accounting education and work in the Philippines. As an emerging global leader in offshore accounting, the Philippines is an ideal context for an exploration of multilingual, multimodal and transnational workplace communication"—Provided by publisher.650 Identifiers: LCCN 2022033598 (print) | LCCN 2022033599 (ebook) | ISBN 9781800416475 (hardback) | ISBN 9781800416482 (pdf) | ISBN 9781800416499 (epub) Subjects: LCSH: Accounting—Study and teaching—Philippines. | Intercultural communication—Philippines. | Business communication—Philippines.
Classification: LCC HF5630 .T38 2023 (print) | LCC HF5630 (ebook) | DDC 657.071/1599—dc23/eng/20221107 LC record available at https://lccn.loc.gov/2022033598
LC ebook record available at https://lccn.loc.gov/2022033599

British Library Cataloguing in Publication Data
A catalogue entry for this book is available from the British Library.

ISBN-13: 978-1-80041-647-5 (hbk)

Multilingual Matters
UK: St Nicholas House, 31–34 High Street, Bristol, BS1 2AW, UK.
USA: Ingram, Jackson, TN, USA.

Website: www.multilingual-matters.com
Twitter: Multi_Ling_Mat
Facebook: https://www.facebook.com/multilingualmatters
Blog: www.channelviewpublications.wordpress.com

Typeset by SAN Publishing Services.

Contents

Acknowledgments

Gifted to give.

I count myself truly rich, having been gifted the golden opportunity to grow in my understanding of language, people and the complex worlds they mutually shape. This book and the research journey that led to its completion are thanks to many people who have generously shared their time, stories, guidance, encouragement, prayers and trust.

Uly, Susan, Theresa, Joseph, and Lanie Tenedero

Aimee Bautista

Distinguished Professor Ingrid Piller and Dr. Loy Lising

The *Language on the Move* reading group

Professor Jo Angouri, Professor Mehdi Boussebaa, and Dr. Caroline Lipovsky

The *Multilingual Matters* team

Ramon and Annie Coloma

The Divine Word Missionaries community in Marsfield, NSW

All the accounting teachers, students, practitioners and employers who have allowed me to enter their world, to see as they see

Your gifts have enabled me to make a gift of this book.

'Every good and perfect gift is from above....' – James 1:17

Transcription and Translation Conventions

Data presented in this book was collected and transcribed in English and Tagalog. As Filipino is based on the Tagalog language, these two language names are typically used interchangeably. In the discussion, the emic term provided by the participants ('Filipino' or 'Tagalog' or 'Filipino/Tagalog') is used.

English translations are provided for the convenience of the reader. All translations are done by me. The Filipino/Tagalog original is presented first, followed by the English translation in brackets.

In transcripts where there is minimal intra-sentential code switching, the English translation is placed immediately after the Filipino/Tagalog expression. Where the code-mixing is more frequent, the complete English translation is provided after the entire code switched excerpt.

Transcription Conventions

Italics	Tagalog text
[Translation]	English translation
(...)	Researcher omission
Bold	Emphatic stress
ah, um	Fillers and hesitation markers
[Comment]	Researcher explanation

1 Introduction

1.1 The Problem of the Accountant Stereotype

Some people describe themselves as good with words but bad with numbers. Others are seen as good with numbers but bad with words. This book is about the second group.

The good-with-numbers-bad-with-words stereotype has been strongly linked to accountants – an ideology that has somehow echoed throughout my career. I am not an accountant. But my training and work have largely involved their profession and this problem of communication persistently built around them.

When I graduated from college with a liberal arts degree, I took a role as an editor and writer for a major accounting firm in one of the central business districts in Metro Manila. My job was to polish reports and letters drafted by accountants, making sure that their work documentation and correspondences were free from grammar, spelling and formatting errors before they were sent to clients. I was the person who did the language work so that the accountants could focus on working the numbers.

As a member of the communications department, I was also part of the company's campaign for excellence, which impelled accountants to produce 'quality in everything [they] do' – including communication. To this end, a handful of us editors were tasked to conduct business writing workshops for newly hired accountants. After the sessions, we gave the participants a list of common errors that we encountered in their work; it was supposed to be a guide in their writing. Yet we continued to track the same syntax and semantic issues in their reports. I wondered whether it was an issue of pedagogy or if – as is typically said of them – accountants really struggle to communicate effectively.

With that question, I took a turn in my career to join academia. Not long after leaving the accounting firm, I started teaching academic writing and oral communication courses in a top-performing accounting school in Manila. Over a decade now in this line of work, I still find myself wondering how effective the communication curriculum in the university is in preparing future accountants for the workplace. Are my lessons relevant to the communication goals in their target workplace? Or am I teaching generic content that is good to know but not really practical?

My interest in students' readiness to communicate at work launched me on a research trajectory focused on exploring communication practices in the accounting field. The more I read, the more I saw that communication in this profession is a persistent, global concern, which is often blamed on the education sector. Accounting students are not motivated enough to develop their communication skills (Kavanagh & Drennan, 2008), partly because they do not see it as valuable in the profession (Ameen, Bruns *et al.*, 2010; Rebele, 1985). They imagine that as accountants they will do more individual than interpersonal work (Lin *et al.*, 2010). Although partly blamed on gaps in the curriculum, these findings also highlight a very personal matter about accountants, specifically, that their views and attitudes toward communication possibly reflect their personality.

Psychometric studies have largely pinned accountants as the type that values numbers more than words. Based on the Holland theory of professional stereotypes, they are 'conventional'; they enjoy working with records in a highly systematic way and have far more superior numerical skills than verbal ability (Aranya *et al.*, 1978). In the extroversion–introversion scale, they are placed as 'stable introverts' who tend to keep to themselves and their books, and do not typically invest in social relations except with people already known to them (Granleese & Barrett, 1990). According to the Myers–Briggs Type Indicator, they are 'sensors/judgers' who are very detail-oriented, orderly and logical (Swain & Olsen, 2012). These descriptors are consistent with the popularized caricature of the 'typical' accountant by American writer Elbert Hubbard (cited in Reves, 1946: 83):

> ...a man past middle age, spare, wrinkled, intelligent, cold, passive, noncommittal, with eyes like a codfish; polite in contact but at the same time unresponsive, calm, and damnably composed as a concrete post or a plaster of Paris cast; a petrification with a heart of feldspar and without charm of the friendly germ, minus bowels, passion, or a sense of humor.

At the risk of discrediting accountants, the stigma of the boring bean-counter image has been challenged. Alternative discourses have been deployed, for instance, through recruitment brochures of the big four accounting firms depicting accountants as cool, adventurous and multitalented (Jeacle, 2008). Another strategy is enlarging the dynamic business consulting role that accountants (in fact, only management accountants) are, occasionally, assigned. However, this business-oriented identity is claimed to be a merely symbolic departure from the traditional bookkeeper role (Morales & Lambert, 2013). Accountants are still mostly confined to number crunching and are more or less still pictured as 'boring grey'.

Concerned and curious about this persistent stereotype, I turned to research for a possible solution. I thought if, as these studies claim, accountants can't help their limited verbal ability because they are internally wired to be so, maybe the answer lies in education! If, as some scholars propose, we properly aligned students' communication training with views and practices in accounting work, then, maybe, this stigma will start to go away. With this vision (or illusion) in mind, I explored what employers and students consider as essential communication skills in accounting work and discovered that, in the Manila context, these two cohorts concurred on the value of interview, reading and communication technology skills (Darang *et al.*, 2015; Tenedero, 2017). I also investigated views and attitudes about speaking, which is claimed to be problematic for accountants (e.g. Ameen, Bruns *et al.*, 2010; Gray, 2010). My findings however indicated that Filipino accounting students are generally confident with the work-readiness of their oral communication skills (Tenedero *et al.*, 2018) and that they do not necessarily experience more communication anxiety than other business majors (Darang *et al.*, 2015).

Up to this point, I have managed to collect Philippine-based evidence against the global 'weak communicator' stereotype levied on accounting students. But I could not reconcile my findings of students' confidence and their teachers' negative views about their communication skills. Accounting and business teachers constantly complained to me and my fellow English language teachers about accounting students' linguistic lapses, from grammar and spelling mistakes, via limited vocabulary, to lack of confidence to speak, and inability to answer in straight English. They turn to us for an explanation for students' poor linguistic performance. Other times, they resign to the belief that, perhaps, because accounting majors have strong numeracy, it is rather normal for them to be verbally handicapped. The stereotype is either called into question as an assumed failure in language instruction or left unchallenged as a normalized part of the target professional identity. The stigma is either 'covered' or 'passed' (Goffman, 1974). But is there another way to manage it? I wondered.

In an attempt to rectify the language problem areas linked to the stereotype, I integrated the findings from my studies into a language for specific purposes unit called *English for Accountants* (Tenedero & Orias, 2016). By explicitly targeting the production of work-relevant communication skills, I had hoped that this curricular innovation would help arrest would-be accountants' communication concerns. Unfortunately, this research-informed unit received a lukewarm reception and up to the time of writing still has not been implemented. This slow uptake, despite the fact that complaints about the poor communication skills of accountants have continued to mount, led me to interrogate more deeply the problem of communication constructed around accountants.

My interest finally shifted from potential solutions to the root of the problem: the deficit discourse. Why are claims about the communication handicap of this occupation group incessantly emphasized in school, at work and in research? Where do they derive legitimacy, so powerful it appears to trivialize evidence contradicting the stereotype? Is curricular alignment with professional practice really the key to this puzzle?

To find more answers, I (re)explored the accounting field.

1.2 Accounting as a Sociolinguistic Site

Though not often recognized as such, accounting represents a relevant context for a sociolinguistic investigation because it is one of the key fields in the expanding global markets of the 21st century, which increasingly involves multilingual, multicultural and transnational communication. Accounting has been identified as a priority skilled occupation in developed countries such as the United States (US), Canada and Australia. In Australia, for example, accounting was in the list of in-demand migrant occupations from 2004 to 2018, remaining 'uncapped' until 2011 (Acharya, 2017; Birrell & Healy, 2008). This open-door policy triggered an influx of international student enrollment in accounting programs and skilled migrants, particularly from developing countries. Reports show that 63,675 overseas accountants migrated to Australia between 2005 and 2012 under the General Skilled Migration program (Weller, 2017). Actual employment outcomes, however, have been less than favorable for this cohort, who are reportedly dispreferred over Australia-born accountants (Costley, 2014; Weller, 2017) and criticized for their purportedly 'inadequate' English and communication skills (Bernard, 2014; Birrell & Healy, 2008; VRL Knowledgebank, 2006). These reports suggest a connection between employability and raciolinguistic background, which highlights the need to explore ideological underpinnings of communication in global accounting practice. It also brings to the fore linguistic and other related challenges confronting migrant workers (see also Piller, 2016, 2017b), particularly those from the Global South.

The known costs and challenges of labor migration are partially addressed through an alternative strategy – process migration, also known as offshore outsourcing, or simply offshoring. This phenomenon involves the international relocation of specific firm activities to a third-party provider instead of relocating workers overseas to the headquarter site (Bals *et al.*, 2013). Part of the attraction of developing countries such as the Philippines as offshoring site is access to qualified professionals who are relatively fluent in English, are information technology (IT) literate, and demand lower salaries than their onshore counterparts (Valanju, 2005).

While the term 'business process outsourcing' (BPO) has been used to describe this practice, I adopt a distinction between BPO, which is more widely linked to customer support through call centers (e.g. Boussebaa *et al.*, 2014; Lockwood, 2012), and knowledge process outsourcing or KPO, which involves higher-end firm activities such as finance and accounting.

This study will focus on KPO, particularly offshore accounting, as a component of globalized accounting.

With its status as one of the most active labor brokerage states exporting workers to different parts of the world since the 1970s (Lorente, 2012) and, more recently, as the second leading offshore location for financial services after India (Valanju, 2005), the Philippines, as a global accounting hub, is a relevant context to explore.

1.3 Globalized Accounting Enterprise in the Philippines

Forms of accounting in the Philippines predate the country's colonial history. Public practice, however, began only after the British occupation of Manila from 1762 to 1763, the earliest public practitioners being the overseas accountants employed by the British who remained in Manila to maintain books of foreign businesses (Apat *et al.*, 2019). Formal training in the field was opened to Filipinos only during the US colonial years from 1898 to 1946. A bookkeeping course, which was first introduced in the US-established Philippine School of Commerce, admitted Filipinos who had completed at least one year of high school and had 'a high level of proficiency in English' (Dyball *et al.*, 2007: 423). Graduates of this program were reportedly in high demand to fill positions in government and business offices from 1911, yet it was only in 1923 that a concrete move to professionalize accounting was made.

Dyball *et al.* (2007: 416) argue that the emergence of the Philippine public accounting profession through the creation of the Board of Accountancy (BoA), sanctioned by Act 3105, was a form of 'professionalization-as-resistance'. They contend that this was essentially the Filipino lawmakers' response to American Insular Auditor's claims that Filipino government accountants at the time were 'financially incompetent' (Dyball *et al.*, 2007: 430). In a move to challenge this negative appraisal, Filipino legislators established the certified public accountant (CPA) identity modeled on US professional certification by creating a law that allowed Filipinos who meet the criteria set by the BoA to be recognized and employed as accounting professionals in public and private offices in the Philippines.

From that time, other initiatives were taken to strengthen the professional status of accounting. This includes the creation of the Philippine Institute of Certified Public Accountants in 1929 and the Professional Regulation Commission in 1973, as well as the subsuming of BoA under the Professional Regulation Commission in 1975. With the expansion of trade relations with North America as well as Europe, the Philippine accounting profession adopted international accounting standards of its overseas business partners, starting with the Generally Accepted Accounting Principles of the US and gradually transitioning to the International Accounting Standards and International Financial

Reporting Standards of Europe in 1996. The local adoption of these international standards were formalized into the Philippine Accounting Standards and the Philippine Financial Accounting Standards in 2004 (Apat *et al.*, 2019).

From the early 2000s, a number of multinational firms from developed economies, such as the US, the United Kingdom (UK), Canada and Australia, began migrating their finance and accounting processes predominantly to Metro Manila, which was seen as the most competitive location of offshoring activities in the Philippines (Kleibert, 2014). This globalized practice of accounting represents the fastest expanding offshore service sector in the country, growing by 525% from 2008 to 2013 (Kleibert, 2015). As one of the biggest global exporters of offshore services, second only to India, the Philippines is seen as an emerging global leader in offshore financial services (Inventor-Miranda, 2008).

Business consultants predict that the global demand for offshore accounting in the Philippines will continue to increase (BusinessMirror, 2017; Inventor-Miranda, 2016). This trend is inevitably changing the way accountants work. For one, offshore jobs provide alternative work arrangements such as the work-from-home option. This and the highly digitized, geographically dispersed, multilingual and intercultural offshore work environment are reshaping the way accountants communicate at work. The salience of communication in offshore accounting translates to discourses enlarging English as 'an important strategic asset' (Kleibert, 2015: 28) as the core language of global business. Yet, in another sense, American business tycoon Warren Buffet claims that 'accounting is the language of business' (Natter, 2018), a necessity for corporate success. While determining whether English or accounting is, in fact, the language of business is not the focus of this book, these parallel notions suggest linguistic connections that I will examine more deeply in the following chapters. To begin to understand the relationship of language practices and accounting in the Philippines, I now turn to a discussion of language policy in education.

1.4 Language Policy and Practice in the Philippines

In the Philippines, language policy in education is largely influenced by prevailing political conditions (Vizconde, 2011, 2017). Prior to colonization, Filipinos used their own local languages or mother tongues, which are estimated to number between 86 and 170 (Almario, 2014). With Spain's 300-year occupation of the archipelago beginning in 1521, the Spanish language was introduced to Filipinos mainly by Catholic religious orders that ran the school system (Rodao, 1997). When the US succeeded in wresting the Philippines from Spain in 1898, the new imperial master introduced the English language, making it the exclusive language of instruction from 1901 to 1974 (Tupas & Tabiola, 2017). This practice is seen as contributing to the dramatic decline in the number of Spanish speakers and increase in English speakers in the country, as indicated in the 1918 and the 1939 Census of the Philippines (Rodao, 1997). Until the US formally relinquished its political sovereignty over the Philippines in 1946, Spanish and English were the only official languages of the land (Sibayan & Gonzalez, 1996).

Part of the agenda for the transition to an independent government was the formation of a national language. In 1939, Manuel Quezon, the then President of the Commonwealth of the Philippines, declared Tagalog (a major language of Central Luzon where the seat of government is located) as the national language. Tagalog was subsequently renamed to 'Pilipino' in 1959 and then 'Filipino' in 1973 (Almario, 2014). The lexical overlap of the national language name (Filipino language) and the word used to indicate nation-state citizenship (Filipino citizen) has the effect of emphasizing the link between language and national identity. It also masks the language's rootedness in Tagalog, which however remains evident in the linguistic features of Filipino. The salience of Tagalog as the basal language of Filipino explains the tendency to use the two language names interchangeably, as is the case in this book.

Since the construction of the national language, English and Filipino have been maintained as official languages of the country. This status is formally documented in the 1974 Bilingual Policy of Education, the 1987 Philippine Constitution and the 2009 Mother Tongue-based Multilingual Education Policy. The latter also encouraged the use of other mother tongues in the early stages of formal schooling. Generally, across primary, secondary and higher education, English and Filipino are taught as language units. Most other units in the curriculum (e.g. maths and sciences) are taught primarily in English, which is the language of textbooks and other instructional materials. The social studies subject in basic education and some culture-bound subjects in higher education (e.g. Philippine literature) adopt Filipino as medium of instruction. However, the dynamics of bilingualism also vary relative to factors such as socioeconomic status and geographical location. In urban-area private schools catering to the upper- and upper-middle classes, English is used more frequently compared with the practice in public schools. With enrollment mostly from lower socioeconomic classes, public school interactions tend to be dominated by Filipino (in urban sites) and other local languages (in regional areas). Meanwhile, in international schools, English is the exclusive medium of instruction for all subjects except for the mandatory Filipino language unit (Sibayan & Gonzalez, 1996).

The coupling of Filipino and English as official languages of governance, education, business, science and media in the Philippines for nearly five decades now has contributed to the emergence of two language varieties: Philippine English and Taglish. Philippine English is the variety of English that has been indigenized in the Philippines.

Primarily focused on usage in 'educated Filipino circles' (Tupas, 2004: 49), as proposed in Llamzon's pioneering paper on 'Standardized Filipino English' in 1969, scholarship in Philippine English has expanded to define the phonological, lexical and syntactic features of the standard (see e.g. Bautista, 2000, 2008) as well as 'less educated' varieties (Bautista, 1982, 1996). Philippine English is distinguished from the Tagalog-English codeswitched variety known as Taglish, which has been recognized as 'a feature of the linguistic repertoire of educated, middle- and upper-class Filipinos' (Bautista, 2004: 226). Although it has been called the 'de facto national language', studies suggest that its use is normative only in higher socioeconomic strata (e.g. Go & Gustilo, 2013).

Taglish and Philippine English are differentially legitimized relative to social context. Taglish, for instance, is sometimes seen as an index of limited proficiency in either Tagalog or English (Bautista, 1999), hence less acceptable in academic discourse. However, investigations also recognize that this codeswitched variety facilitates the transfer of Tagalog elements into the Manila-centric variety of Philippine English, which is increasingly gaining acceptance in academia (Lising *et al.*, 2020). Local studies in English language teaching are actively exploring ways to make Philippine English part of the 'pedagogical backbone in teaching and learning the English language' (Bernardo, 2022; see also Bernardo, 2017; Bernardo & Madrunio, 2015), which are traditionally oriented toward the American English variety. Interest in using the Philippine English version as a model for English language instruction in the country challenges the hegemonic ideology favoring nativism.

The key point here is that, regardless of proclivity for native or non-native standard, English maintains a broad social legitimacy as the language of economic opportunity and social mobility. It is designated as the language of professional domains, which is indicated, for instance, in its use as medium of the licensing examination (Sibayan & Gonzalez, 1996). This privileged position is further reinforced by its instrumentality in transnational employment through labor migration and offshoring (Lorente, 2017).

The high value of English also holds in the accounting profession, of course (Sibayan & Gonzalez, 1996). That English is the self-evident and obvious language of accounting in the Philippines was confirmed in a brief exchange I had with one of my neighbors who had worked as an accountant for many years. She was curious about my research. Simply, I said I'm investigating how globalized accountants communicate at work. With a visibly faded interest, she told me the answer in a matter-of-fact way – 'English!'

This book demonstrates that this seemingly obvious answer is part of the problem of the communication stereotype with which I opened this chapter.

1.5 Outline of the Book

This book examines the ideological underpinnings of the deficit discourse circulating about the communication skills of Filipino accountants which are widely blamed on the communication training they receive in university. Across seven chapters, I gradually uncover (dis)connections between communication practices and ideologies in the domains of accounting education and accounting workplaces.

Following this introductory chapter is an overview of the current state of knowledge on communication in accounting (Chapter 2). This discussion situates my research in the under-represented area of Global South epistemology on literacy and oracy practices and understandings across the education-to-workplace continuum of a professional discipline. I also discuss the sociolinguistic-ethnographic approach used to contribute some new knowledge in this area.

The back-to-back investigation of the interrelated but often separately explored domains of education and work is presented in two parts. Part 1 focuses on the education domain – how curricular documents construct communication as an expected graduate attribute (Chapter 3) and whether and how entextualized notions of 'good communication' are enacted in the classroom (Chapter 4). The analysis of interactional data foregrounds tensions between present academic and future professional aspirations, hierarchical positioning of English and Filipino as language of knowledge and rapport, and the differential valuing of practitioner and academic teacher advice on how to communicate effectively.

Part 2 zooms in on the work domain – how communication skills are tied to the image of an employable accountant in online job ads (Chapter 5) and what on-the-ground practices intersect with language use, policy and ideologies of globalized accountants (Chapter 6). Some highlights are the explicit and implicit styling of the way accountants communicate on the job, and the digitization of communication in a highly technology-dependent work environment. Overall, the findings show that communication is mutually shaped by different stakeholders (or 'social agents' in sociolinguistic terms) for diverse purposes. This includes the performance of global competence and local identity, ritualistic compliance with institutional norms of communication, and agentive ways of coping with practices that disadvantage their language proficiencies and challenge their ideologies of what makes communication good.

Chapter 7 synthesizes the key findings of this investigation and highlights some practical and theoretical contributions in accounting and in sociolinguistics. This closing chapter demystifies the persistent stereotyping of accountants as poor communicators by drawing attention to the taken-for-granted ways that this social construct is (re)produced rhetorically and interactionally in academia and the profession. The proposed curricular innovations and sociolinguistic understandings of this phenomenon aim to shift the tenor of the conversation from the perennial shaming of accountants' linguistic insecurity to the recognition of how they strategically and ideologically navigate language work in their number-centric job.

2 Communication in Global Education and Work: What We Know

2.1 Professional Necessity for Accounting Success

That communication is important in the accounting profession is old news. For over half a century now, it has been recognized that the work of accountants is not only to measure financial and economic data but also to communicate them meaningfully to decision makers (Carey, 1965; Littleton & Zimmerman, 1962). This view is echoed in the 1986 Report by the Bedford Committee on the Future Structure, Content and Scope of Accounting Education; the 1989 White Paper of the Big 8 Accounting Firms; and the 1994 Institute of Management Accountants Report. Also emphasized in these reports is the role of higher education in preparing accounting students to communicate professionally (Anderson, 2013). After all, who else would be responsible for the subpar communication skills of newly graduated accountants (see Andrews & Sigband, 1984; Zaid & Abraham, 1994)?

Increasing curricular pressure to develop the 'professional necessity' that is communicative competence, Roy and MacNeill (1970: 41) recommended screening the English language skills of would-be accountants in the professional examination and denying license to those with inadequate linguistic ability. This plan materialized beginning May 1994 when the American Institute of Certified Public Accountants included writing skills in the qualifying criteria for the professional exam (VanZante & Person, 1994). This move was adapted in 2015 by the Professional Regulatory Board of Accountancy in the Philippines, mandating the inclusion of English grammar items in the certified public accountants (CPA) board exam.

Arguably contributing to the sharpened focus on accountants' writing is the high-profile accounting scandals in the US in the early 2000s, which put accountant-authored documents in the spotlight. Bhatia's (2008: 166) critical genre analysis of Enron's annual financial report exposes the 'use and abuse of linguistic and rhetorical strategies' in corporate disclosure documents that simultaneously communicate accounting, economic, public relations and legal discourses (see also Bhatia, 2010).

The deficit discourse highlighted in these events and earlier studies concerning global finance fueled further investigations into accounting communication. A marked priority in this scholarship is defining what constitutes effective communication in the field. The notion has been variably linked to career level (Boyle *et al.*, 2014; Christensen & Rees, 2002), to generic, 'soft' skills (Weaver & Kulesza, 2014), and to more specific abilities such as speaking (e.g. Ameen, Bruns *et al.*, 2010), listening (Gray & Murray, 2011; Stone & Lightbody, 2012), writing (Jones, 2011; Nellermoe *et al.*, 1999) and demonstrating English proficiency across these macro skills (Suttipun, 2012).

These studies foreground the ambiguity of the desired communication skills of practitioners despite the general consensus on its necessity 'for success in a career in today's business/accounting world' (Kavanagh & Drennan, 2008: 296). Different stakeholders – quite unsurprisingly – have multiple (even contradictory) views about what communication skills accountants need to prioritize and how these skills can best be taught. So while offering some answers about the communication question, diverse understandings of effective communication in accounting also enlarge the gaps discourse that already pervades literature.

Another trend that stands out is the predominant situatedness of these studies in the US, Australia and the UK. I believe this is partly due to the predominant coloniality of knowledge that places Anglocentric scholarship on a pedestal. Thanks to the significantly Anglophone academic publishing regime (Piller, 2010), articles by scholars in the US, Australia and the UK contexts are more easily accessible. Of course, this does not mean that no scholar outside the Anglosphere has ever written on the subject. This research context pattern, however and unfortunately, has the effect of implicitly designating the Global North as authority in matters of global professional communication.

A laudable effort to shift this status quo is the 2018 Special Issue of *Accounting, Auditing, and Accountability Journal*, which spotlights cultures and languages other than English that are less prominent in the accounting research agenda. The featured articles highlight issues in the global project of translating accounting standards from English to other mother tongues, which is largely taken for granted as a straightforward, technical activity because of the view that English is a neutral language (Evans, 2018; Evans & Kamla, 2018; Kamla & Komori, 2018). These critical studies bring to the fore power inequalities tied to multilingualism in a largely Englishized accounting world (Detzen & Loehlein, 2018). They also awaken readers to the reality that other languages, not just English, matter in the transnational practice of accounting (e.g. Kettunen, 2017).

That less central languages in the global language system (de Swaan, 2001) are largely left out in conversations about global professional communication points to an important gap that this book speaks to. Limited studies in the role of peripheral languages and predominance of research focused on English in global professional contexts are evidence, too, of neoliberal ideologies in higher education and corporate work.

2.2 Object of Neoliberal Governance

Adopting Bourdieu's (1990) concept of capital, linguistic skills are seen as an asset that can be transubstantiated; they index knowledge and are, in turn, assigned economic, cultural, social and symbolic value (Moore, 2014: 102). This view of communication as capital fits into the neoliberal framework that emphasizes economic and symbolic capital that creates distinctions on the basis of power and mobility (Kirilova & Angouri, 2017; Urciuoli & LaDousa, 2013). With this focus, the way schools and workplaces operate is subordinated to the economic agenda so that students and workers are seen as a 'bundle of skills' (Urciuoli, 2008: 211), a product with a set of features that are advertised as value-adding in the highly competitive, global job market. Not least among these valued skills is global communicative competence, which is strongly linked to proficiency in English, the designated language of globalization (Louhiala-Salminen & Kankaanranta, 2011).

Where this connection originated and how it continues to thrive are traced to the education system, the 'delegated authority [that] engage[s] in a universal process of durable inculcation in matters of language' (Bourdieu & Thompson, 1992: 63). Teachers are seen as influencers of language ideologies, powerfully shaping the linguistic practices, views and dispositions of students (Moore, 2014). This is exemplified by the use of English as the main medium of instruction accompanied by curricular rhetoric of economic benefit (Parba, 2018), employability (Blackmore *et al.*, 2017), social mobility (Jenkins, 2017) and global competitiveness (Piller & Cho, 2013). Steeped in these mantras over time, students learn to assign superiority to English, especially native varieties, and prefer using it 'purely' as opposed to mixing with other languages (Gu, 2014). Learners continue to hold these views despite suffering the consequences of English-only assessments that disadvantage those who have a different first language (King *et al.*, 2021).

Critical research has further problematized these decontextualized discourses of benefit that overstate the affordances of English proficiency (Holborow, 2018; Ricento, 2018), which accrue differentially. The fact is, even when they are able to use the legitimized forms of English, individuals marked by non-English names and/or non-native English accents (Lippi-Green, 2012; Piller, 2016) and/or racialized bodies (Flores & Rosa, 2015) have been deemed deficient and consequently disadvantaged in the opportunity market. This injustice foregrounds the inconsistency between the overly simplistic academic rhetoric equating English proficiency with better earnings and the reality of unequal transubstantiation of language into a form of capital in transnational contexts – an issue largely ignored in language-in-education policy formation (Lorente, 2017).

The persistent 'grip of English', which Lorente (2012: 196) described in the Philippine context, has been identified as a force restraining teachers from enacting their positive views about the value of languages other than English in instruction (Henderson, 2017). This condition relates to Bourdieu's concern about the 'socially (re)productive effects of formal education' in institutionalizing standards of eliteness (Thomson, 2014: 76), reinforcing a monolingual habitus (Ellis *et al.*, 2010), devaluing multilingualism (Lorente, 2017) and inflating the utilitarian value of English in work contexts (e.g. Piller & Takahashi, 2013).

Mirroring the regime of language control and English hegemony in the academia, workplaces have become sites for language management. Scrutiny of workers' language is most obvious in gatekeeping practices such as job interviews, where candidates' fluency in English serves as an abstract, underspecified, but powerful criterion for hiring decisions (Lockwood, 2012; Roberts, 2013). The positioning of English as the centerpiece of the selection process reflects and reproduces post-colonial power dynamics of domination by the Anglosphere and subordination of former colonies (Boussebaa *et al.*, 2014).

Once hired, workers have their language continually checked through such approaches as the prescription of a workplace lingua franca, such as a policy for monolingual English (e.g. Piller & Takahashi, 2013) and occupation-specific linguistic structuring as in the vocal styling of call center workers (Boussebaa *et al.*, 2014; Cameron, 2000b) and the scripting of migrant domestic workers (Lorente, 2018). Explicit training and increased investment in corporate communication contribute to the standardization of language where trainers play a key role in prescribing norms and codifying ideal communication practices in the workplace (Cameron, 2002; Del Percio, 2018).

A dominant ideal embedded in these language management practices privileges native varieties of English as the 'pure' or 'perfect' variety (e.g. Boussebaa *et al.*, 2014). This distinction is patently foregrounded in contexts that bring together native and non-native varieties of English (Salonga, 2010), such as transnational work where non-native speakers are styled to sound American or British. Yet, even with critical studies challenging this category of performance (Kirilova & Angouri, 2017), the native speaker benchmark continues to be a powerful standard for language use in globalized settings.

Collectively, these sociolinguistic studies demonstrate an important link between communication and a neoliberal motivation that constructs particular language skills as a key capital in the global market. This strong ideological connection is possibly related to the persistence of the deficit discourse as regards the communication skills of Global South accountants. With native, Global North English as the gold standard of transnational professional communication, no wonder Global South speakers of English are perpetually deemed inadequate. How Filipino globalized accountants navigate this discriminatory standard is part of my research. The answer partly lies in the view of communication practices as performance.

2.3 Site for Identity Performance

The view of language practices as performance shifts the focus on communication from ability (competence) to how it is shaped in context (Bauman, 1992). Language practice is seen as a social phenomenon, the product of cultural embodiment and discursive forces on site. Language-as-performance studies explore 'all the activity of a given participant on a given occasion which serves to influence in any way any of the other participants' (Goffman, 1990: 26). This definition of performance, which I adopt in my analysis, encompasses language practices in the 'front region' as well as the 'back region' (Goffman, 1990: 114). The former is where desirable impressions (competence, professionalism) are created in ritualized fashion for ratified (employer, customers) and unratified (overhearers) listeners. The latter is the space where, away from the hearing of a judging audience, social actors may collude to contradict front stage impressions (see also Goffman, 1981).

While this lens begins with recognizing social context as a formative force in communication, it also examines the agentive role of social actors in discursively (re)constructing communication practices within conditions of regulation. This emphasizes 'the productive force of language in constituting identity rather than identity being a pregiven construct that is reflected in language use' (Pennycook, 2004: 13).

From this point of view, compliance with linguistic regulation may be construed as a device for corporate identity construction and impression management. Specific ways of talking can produce positive (or negative) impressions, thereby rationalizing socially created rules about 'correct' language use. Following these protocols is widely explored in studies analyzing participants' linguistic choices in events where some form of economic and symbolic distinction is at stake. An example is the job interview, a language game (Blackmore *et al.*, 2017; Roberts, 2013) that involves linguistically performing impressions of expertness (Lipovsky, 2006), affiliation (Lipovsky, 2008) and integration (Holmes, 2007).

Individual workers' linguistic compliance is also viewed as contributing to building a standard organizational image, also known as 'branding' (Cameron, 2000b), which has been used to rationalize formal language policy (Piller & Takahashi, 2013). In relation to policies, research on surveillance practices, which examines how individuals and organizations are treated as 'subjects of audit' (Power, 1994: 3), problematizes the artificiality of the 'enhanced performance' (Strathern, 2000: 72) induced by the anxious desire to please a ratified audience, whose watchful gaze scrutinizes and rewards (or penalizes) their performance based on unquestioned indicators of excellence.

Further probing ideologies undergirding compliance, language management may not exclusively be oriented toward satisfying the language managers (Butler, 1997). It is also a potential site for the performance of alternative identities. What may appear to be quiet subordination may be, in some cases, a strategic move to gain some form of social advantage. Building on James Scott's (1985) notion of 'weapons of the weak', Canagarajah (2000: 122) refers to these 'half-hearted acts' as 'false compliance' or 'strategies by which the marginalized detach themselves from the ideologies of the powerful, retain a measure of critical thinking, and gain some sense of control over their life in an oppressive situation'.

This form of agency is particularly salient in contexts where communication issues are foregrounded in work routines and outcomes, as is the case in offshore call center work. In this transnational context involving daily interactions with customers from an Anglosphere background, non-Anglosphere call center workers are heavily styled and monitored to speak 'perfect English' (Salonga, 2010: 218), which is code for native standard. The vocal styling of the worker is viewed as a means to construct a 'single corporate persona' (Cameron, 2000a: 101), a standardized embodiment of 'good customer service' which is linked with feminized speech style (Cameron, 2000b: 337). While participating in this verbal mimicry, customer service representatives variably express resistance to the 'perfect English' discourse, which devalues the kind of English they bring into the workplace. They enact this opposition by codeswitching, producing hybrid linguistic forms (Boussebaa *et al.*, 2014), even 'bastardizing' English through 'deliberate pidginization' (Salonga, 2010: 229) when speaking among themselves. This back stage action is construed as a form of subversion, a subtle challenging of the English hegemony by 'creating out-of-sight spaces' where they can exercise control over their own language use (Boussebaa *et al.*, 2014: 1163).

In these studies of restrictive and creative intersections of languages in work contexts, centralized varieties of English are typically depicted as performative of global identity, especially one that bears the likeness of Anglosphere eliteness. Meanwhile, the use of peripheral varieties of English, other languages, language mixing and accent shifting are strategies linked to deemphasizing a global persona, revealing nation-state affinity, even strategically constructing a 'multilayered identity' that concurrently embodies metropolitan and regional belongingness (Dong &

Blommaert, 2009: 20) or global and local appeal (Heller & Duchêne, 2012; Lorente, 2012). Critical discourse analysts, however, caution against 'simplistic dichotomization' (Pennycook, 2000b: 64). Simply equating English with globalness and heritage language with localness loses sight of the complex intersection between language and dominant social, cultural, economic and political discourses in international and local contexts (Pennycook, 2000a, 2007).

Overall, scholarship in language as performance highlights connections between proficiency, identity and embodiment. As Piller (2017a: 97) argues, 'our linguistic proficiencies constrain the identities we can perform, at the same time, our embodied identities constrain the ways in which our linguistic performances are perceived'. Although variably restricted, communication is also identified as a creative site for the formation, negotiation and intersection of institutional and individual identities. By spotlighting some back stage performances, this book contributes to the understanding of communication as a phenomenon that is simultaneously corporate and personal.

2.4 Expanding What We Know

So far, communication has been studied as not just a static, commodified skill but also an active commodifying object and performative site. Some spaces in this conversation, however, have been little explored. For one, there is a glaring imbalance in the knowledge produced on the subject, which so far has largely represented Anglocentric, Global North perspectives. What is known today about communication in globalized accounting is mostly Global North-informed and, therefore, not 'global' enough. As accountants from the underexplored, offshore context are growing in their participation in the field, it is becoming more and more critical to provide Global South representations on what counts as 'good' communication in accounting.

In this book, I adopt the term 'Global South' to refer to 'developing' or 'third-world' countries such as the Philippines. While the North–South distinction demarcated by the Brandt line oversimplifies global power and economic relations, it is an important construct that shapes how the Global South is imagined (Williams, 2011), often as 'places and peoples in need of external (i.e. Northern) intervention' (Williams *et al.*, 2014: 3). My focus is on the problem of 'poor' communication, which is persistently tied to accountants born and educated in the Philippines. I argue that this negative label originates from a largely Global North standard of 'good' communication.

Another tendency in sociolinguistic research on language as performance is to focus on speech rather than written discourse. The attention to oracy may be linked to the sociolinguistic prejudice against written language (Coulmas, 2013) and the salience of ideologies linked to phonological features of oral language performance, such as accent. Although perhaps less accessible to researchers, written interactions (e.g. email) also potentially reflect ideologies that may have important implications in literacy training.

Finally, sociolinguistic studies tend to be selectively situated either in education or in work settings. There seems to be little, if any, attempt to explore communication ideologies and practices across the education-profession continuum. The growing literature on call center work (e.g. Boussebaa *et al.*, 2014; Salonga, 2010) suggests increasing interest in transnational work conducted offshore, which Shome (2006: 116) described as a kind of 'virtual migration', where workers are simultaneously operating in two territories while physically situated in one. An emerging form of virtual migration is offshore accounting work, where the pragmatic centrality of communication is not easily visible or recognized, making it a novel site for investigating language work. To the best of my knowledge, this is the first sociolinguistic study exploring (dis)continuities in language ideologies and practices across the education and work domains of globalized accounting.

I define globalized accounting as the training for and practice of accounting that supports global businesses. The scope of this field includes accounting education and work institutions that are based overseas as well as those situated locally but with international linkages and/or potential trajectories for globalized employment. This definition recognizes that local practices in accounting education and work are tied to globalized aspirations and opportunities. In other words, what makes the field globalized is not so much the physical location of the university or workplace as the globalized trajectories and aspirations of accounting students and professionals, who occupy these spaces. This underexplored research territory is the context of the study presented in this book.

The discussion following this chapter is organized into two parts: Part 1 examines spoken and written practices and ideologies in schools; Part 2 explores the workplaces. Sociolinguistic ethnography provides a framework to critically examine how and why language is mobilized in these domains represented by two top-performing accounting universities and 11 workplaces of globalized accountants in Metro Manila. As an interpretive, grounded analysis of the mutual shaping of language and context, this approach defamiliarizes accounting, proposing that the characteristically numbers-centric field is also a site for important global, multilingual communication and that accountants are also language workers, except that this part of their occupation is largely invisible.

Table 2.1 summarizes the ethnographic data I collected over a four-month fieldwork in the Philippines in 2018, which I analyze in this study. The profile of the participants is provided in the Appendix.

Table 2.1 Ethnographic data

Data type	Description
Observation field notes	30 field notes covering 32 hours of observations
Interviews	39 interviews equivalent to 14 hours of audio recordings
Documents	231 curricular documents, 135 online job advertisements, 88 work emails by accountants, 12 communication activity logs

What do these data sets indicate about how accountants are trained to communicate? The next chapter begins exploring this question.

Part 1

Communication in Accounting Education

3 The Discourse of 'Effective Communication' in the Curriculum

3.1 Introduction

In this chapter, I explore communication practices and ideologies in accounting education as reflected in documents gathered from the higher education government agency and two top-performing accounting schools in Metro Manila. I investigate how 'communication' is discursively constructed by accounting education authorities represented by these institutions.

Using a top-down approach, I first examine policy documents produced by the Commission on Higher Education (CHED) regulating accountancy programs offered by higher education institutions in the Philippines. Then, I review next curricular documents created by academic administrators and teachers. The selected universities consistently ranked among the highest in the certified public accountants (CPA) board exams from 2015 to 2017. Both identified schools are private, coeducational universities run by Catholic religious orders offering undergraduate and graduate degrees in their Manila-based campuses.

With the timing of this research coinciding with the transition into a new curriculum for the Bachelor of Science major in Accountancy (BSA) program, I included in the analysis relevant documents pertaining to both the 2007 (also referred to as 'old') and 2018 ('new') BSA curricula. This inclusion criterion enables a glimpse into shifts, if any, in communication training rhetoric and design.

Table 3.1 shows the documents included in the analysis, representing different levels of accounting education authority – government framework level, institutional program level and unit level.

To contextualize this analysis of curricular documents, I begin with an overview of major reforms in the Philippine education system that precipitated changes in the BSA program (Section 3.2). This background is followed by a corpus analysis of the positioning of 'communication' in the structure of the documents (Section 3.3) and the dominant rhetoric on

Table 3.1 Curricular documents for accounting education

Document type	2007 BSA curriculum	2018 BSA curriculum
Government guidelines	CHED Memorandum Order 03, series of 2007	CHED Memorandum Order 27, series of 2017
Program prospectus	BSA program prospectus	BSA program prospectus
Course descriptions	BSA course descriptions	BSA course descriptions

what counts as 'effective communication' (Section 3.4). Finally, I summarize the consistencies, tensions and shifts in the discursive construction of communication in this domain (Section 3.5).

3.2 Accounting Education Reforms in the Philippines

The accounting curriculum in the Philippines has evolved along with changes in the Philippine education system. An important reform in the Philippine education system, which came into effect around the time of this investigation, is the K to 12 program, also known as the Enhanced Basic Education Act of 2013 or Republic Act No. 10533, ratified by the then President Benigno Aquino III on 15 May 2013.

The law sanctioned an overhaul of the country's basic education system in two ways: one is the medium of instruction, where the use of the mother tongues in the early grade levels is prescribed; another is the time component. Two years were added to the former 10-year basic education cycle, which had been criticized as insufficient preparation period for students to master necessary competencies for positive employment outcomes (Kleibert, 2015). Benchmarking against international education standards, the mandatory pre-university education timeline now consists of one year of Kindergarten (K), six years of elementary school (Grades 1 to 6), four years of junior high school (Grades 7 to 10) and two years of senior high school (Grades 11 and 12). This new framework entailed the creation of new curriculum guides by the Department of Education, which are touted as superior to the old curricula and as 'decongested, seamless, relevant and responsive, enriched, and learner-centered' (DepEd Resources, 2017: para. 2).

In addition to the core curriculum, senior high school students are given the choice among four tracks: (1) academic, (2) technical-vocational livelihood, (3) arts and design and (4) sports. Tracks two, three and four are options for those intending to apply for jobs after completing Grade 12, while track one is for those who wish to pursue a bachelor's degree. The academic track gives students further options among four strands matched to their target bachelor's degree: (1) accountancy, business and management; (2) science, technology, engineering and mathematics; (3) humanities and social sciences; and (4) general academic. High school students who intend to do a bachelor's in accountancy, for instance, are advised to take up accountancy, business and management.

Both universities that served as research sites for this study began offering this high school accountancy academic track in 2016. In doing this, they expanded their academic program offerings, which now includes the senior high school diploma, in addition to various undergraduate and graduate degrees. This strategy provides the opportunity to attract senior high school graduates into a related bachelor's program offered in the same institution.

This change demonstrates the impact of the K to 12 program on the higher education sector, which also had to effect significant curricular reforms to complement changes in basic education. The key changes in the tertiary education curriculum are the adoption of the outcomes-based education approach used in primary and secondary education, the reduction of the general education courses from 63 (or 51 for science and math majors) to 36 units, and the allocation of more curricular space for specialization or professional courses (Commission on Higher Education [CHED], n.d.).

The technical committee appointed by the CHED for each field of specialization determines the other mandatory curricular requirements. In the case of accountancy, the Accounting Education Technical Committee, in collaboration with the Board of Accountancy, are jointly responsible for deciding on the professional courses to be included in the new BSA program. In modifying the 2007 BSA curriculum, they considered the K to 12 reforms, the new general education curriculum, alignment of the Philippine qualification framework with that of other ASEAN member countries, revisions of the international education standards in accounting education, and qualification standards of new globally recognized certifying bodies (BOA Admin, 2015). Accounting education providers consequently rolled out the new BSA curriculum to first-year students from the academic year 2018–2019 onward.

It is at this transition phase to the new BSA curriculum that I entered the field as a researcher. This timing facilitated my access to newly updated curricular documents and afforded me the opportunity to evaluate whether and how new policies and plans are translated into teaching on the ground (see Chapter 4). As an initial step to understanding communication practices in accounting education, I begin by examining how education authorities construct the rhetoric of 'communication' in official documents.

3.3 The Place of Communication in the Accounting Curriculum

3.3.1 'Communication' at government framework level

As a government agency, the primary mandate of CHED published in its official website (https://ched.gov.ph/ched/) is 'to promote relevant and

Table 3.2 Placement of 'communication' in government guidelines for the BSA curriculum

CHED MO 03, series of 2007	CHED MO 27, series of 2017
Article 1 – Introduction	Article 1 – Introduction
Article 2 – Authority to operate	Article 2 – Authority to operate
Article 3 – Program specifications	Article 3 – General provisions
Article 4 – Competency standards	**Article 4 – Program specifications**
Article 5 – Administration	**Article 5 – Curriculum**
Article 6 – Faculty	Article 6 – Required resources
Article 7 – Curriculum	Article 7 – Compliance of higher education institutions
Article 8 – Library	Article 8 – Transitory, repealing and effectivity provisions
Article 9 – Instructional standards	Annex A – Bachelor of science in accountancy sample course syllabus in Intermediate Accounting III
Article 10 – Admission and retention standards	
Article 11 – Research	
Article 12 – Linkages with other schools, business establishments, public sector (government agencies) and accounting practitioners	
Article 13 – Standards of performance for graduates	
Article 14 – Effectivity	
Article 15 – Repealing clause	
Article 16 – Sanctions	
Annex A – Suggested course description, course outline, and references	
Annex B – Sample program of study for the minimum units	
Annex C – Flowchart showing course sequencing and their pre-requisites	

quality higher education'. To realize this goal, one of its powers and functions is to 'set minimum standards for programs and institutions of higher learning'. In the case of accounting education, CHED issued Memorandum Order 03, series of 2007 and Memorandum Order 27, series of 2017 to identify the minimum requirements for the BSA programs offered from 2007 and from 2018, respectively. Table 3.2 shows the overall structure of the two government documents. Highlighted are the sections where 'communication' is mentioned.

The positioning of 'communication' in specific sections of the documents indicates the curricular value ascribed to it. While the earlier guideline has more varied iterations, both documents identify communication as a target competency and as a curricular component.

Examining Article 4 of both documents, I find that while they are differently titled, they similarly discuss the expected attributes of accountancy graduates. The 2007 text refers to these target attributes as 'core competencies' or the 'knowledge, skill, and values that the BSA graduate should possess'. In parallel, the 2017 guideline refers to 'program outcomes', which is presented as a checklist of skills and tasks that graduates are expected to be able to demonstrate. In these descriptions, the ideal accounting graduate is distinguished through literacy, oracy and language proficiencies.

First of all, 'effective' communication is defined in the guidelines in terms of oral and written expression. These notions are highlighted below in the 2007 document:

> This [communication] refers to active listening skills and the ability to communicate effectively one's points of view, **both orally and in writing,** at all organizational levels; being able to justify one's position, **deliver impressive presentations** and to persuade and convince others. The BSA graduate should demonstrate skills such as the ability to:
>
> - **Explain verbally and/or in writing** financial/statistical/administrative matters/policies/procedures/regulatory matters/audit results at a level appropriate to the audience.
> - Ask clear, concise and relevant questions to obtain desired information to perform a task.
> - Negotiate effectively. (Article 4, Section 18, emphasis mine)

Comparably, the 2017 guideline states that a graduate of a business or management degree (such as BSA) is expected to be able, *inter alia*, to 'express clearly and communicate effectively with stakeholders **both in oral and written forms**' (Article 4, Section 6.2, emphasis mine).

References to literacy and oracy as marks of university education is banal. It is important to note, however, that the use-value of these generic skills in accounting work contexts ('at all organizational levels' and 'with stakeholders') is highlighted in the guidelines. This reflects the orientation of education toward employment goals, which is also evident in the introduction of the 2007 framework:

> Increasingly, today's professional accountants need to be **technical experts with excellent communication skills.** ... In addition to acquiring technical accounting knowledge and skills, professional accountants need skills that enable them to be, when appropriate, business advisors, financial analysis, **communicators**, negotiators, and managers. (Article 1, Section 3, emphasis mine)

The valuing of students' ability in written and spoken communication in connection with their potential roles in the accounting workplace is further examined in Chapter 4.

With regard to linguistic competence, the two policy documents reflect differential priority for English and Filipino. The 2007 memorandum cites 'competency in the English language (the lingua franca of business)' as a trait that 'will make our Filipino CPAs prominent in the global marketplace' (Article 4, Section 17). Meanwhile, the 2017 document states that graduates should have the ability to 'effectively communicate...using both English and Filipino' (Article 4, Section 6.1). In both policy statements, English is mentioned as the medium for effective communication.

This idea, however, is visibly foregrounded in the earlier document's reference to English as the lingua franca of international business.

Further emphasizing the value of English in relation to the business sector, the 2007 guideline calls for the inclusion of an English language requirement as a proviso for acceptance to the BSA program.

> As part of the admission requirements to the Accountancy Program, students should meet an English language requirement to be set by the College/Department. An English Proficiency test shall therefore be given to all applicants and those who fail to meet the grade requirement will need to undergo an English Bridging Program (e.g. English 0).
>
> English 0 is a course that bridges the gap between the freshmen's previous English language qualifications and those conditionally accepted in the Accountancy Program. The course provides a cultural context for developing language skills, content knowledge and autonomous learning. Classes focus on academic skills and preparation for the reading, writing, speaking and listening, note-taking and research that the students will be undertaking in the program.
>
> The program is a 40-hour program taken during the first curriculum year of the program preferably during the summer prior enrolling in the Program. If the student successfully completes this program, he is admitted to the Accountancy Program. (Article 10, Section 50)

The condition to administer a language proficiency test and to require those who fail it to complete a bridging course are found only in the 2007 document. It strongly links the ability to communicate in English with the accounting discipline, making it a criterion for official and conditional admission to the program. This gatekeeping function implies that English proficiency is a standard measure of worthiness to join the BSA program and, later, the accounting profession. In other words, acceptance to the field is seen as partially contingent on the English language proficiency of potential students.

This dominant monolingual ideation, however, appears somewhat de-emphasized in the 2017 policy document, which proposes bilingualism in English and Filipino as the ideal linguistic competence of accountancy graduates. I shall revisit this shift in linguistic focus later.

In addition to defining communication in terms of written and spoken communication and proficiency in English and Filipino, the government guidelines also identify the place of communication training in the BSA program. The curriculum section of both policy statements (Article 7 in 2007 and Article 5 in 2017) define general education as the component that 'focuses on the development of nonprofessional knowledge, intellectual skills, personal skills, interpersonal and communication skills'. The core competencies identified in general education are communication, logical and critical thinking, and quantitative reasoning. Focusing on developing skills that are broadly relevant rather than tied to specific professions reflects the priority of liberal arts education to develop 'well-rounded global citizens' (Jiang, 2014: 1). Where students are enrolled in nonliberal arts degrees, such as accounting, this pedagogic goal is targeted in general education subjects, suggesting that the harnessing of communicative ability is the province of the general curriculum.

Table 3.3 compares the prescribed units in the general education curriculum based on the 2007 and the 2017 policy statements. Highlighted are the units that provide explicit instruction to develop communication skills.

As shown in the table, the 2007 curriculum prescribed a minimum of four language courses (two English and two Filipino), which has been reduced to one mandatory communication course in the new curriculum. The focus of Purposive Communication is developing students' ability in 'writing, speaking, and presenting to different audiences and for various

Table 3.3 General education units prescribed in 2007 and 2017 CHED policies for BSA

2007 CHED policy		**2017 CHED policy**	
Course title	**Units**	**Course title**	**Units**
Communication Skills 1	3	Understanding the Self	3
Communication Skills 2	3	Readings in Philippine History	3
Sining ng Pakikipagtalastasan [Art of Communication Skills]	3	The Contemporary World	3
Pagbasa/ Pagsulat sa Iba't Ibang Disiplina [Reading/Writing in Different Disciplines]	3	Mathematics in the Modern World	3
Philippine Literature	3	**Purposive Communication**	3
Introduction to Philosophy with Logic and Critical Thinking	3	Art Appreciation	3
Art, Man, and Society	3	Science, Technology, and Society	3
College Algebra	3	Ethics	3
Mathematics of Investment	3	Rizal's Life and Works	3
Physical Science	3	Electives (e.g. Business Logic)	9
Biological Science	3		
Fundamentals of Computer Software and Applications	3		
Philippine History with Politics and Governance	3		
Society and Culture with Family Planning	3		
General Psychology	3		
Introduction to Economics with Land Reform and Taxation	3		
Life and Works of Rizal	3		
Total	51		36

purposes' (CHED, 2013: 13). This scope resembles that of the English and Filipino units in the old general curriculum, which have been devolved to the senior high school core curriculum. However, as this unit may be optionally offered by universities in Filipino as *Malayuning Komunikasyon* [Purposive Communication], it indicates a shift from a language-specific to a more skills- and context-focused orientation to communication training. Beyond units where communication training is explicit, the other general education courses are also intended to prepare students to develop their communication abilities, as well as other core competencies. How different units incorporate communication in the course design is further discussed in Section 3.3.3.

Overall, government policies construct 'effective communication' as a desired graduate attribute that is reflected in the ability to speak and write in English and Filipino. As a pedagogical target, it is positioned as a priority of the general education curriculum, which is oriented toward producing generic skills that are applicable in various domains. This practice reflects the ideology that 'higher education should produce workers and that the content of education should justify the investment of time and expense by being a practical help for the job market' (Urciuoli, 2014: 79). In producing work-ready graduates, the general education (comparable to liberal arts) curriculum is constructed as a site for the (re)production of communication skills that are broadly relevant in the job market (Urciuoli, 2014) but also specifically valued in globalized accounting practice.

3.3.2 'Communication' at program level

The government guidelines examined in the previous section serve as a basis for the accounting schools' program prospectus, a formal document providing more specific details about the BSA degree, including expected graduate attributes, program objectives and target learning outcomes. Where 'communication' figures in these program documents is shown in Table 3.4.

Immediately salient is the positioning of 'communication' in the university graduate attribute section of both prospectuses. This aligns with the practice at the government level. To probe the institutional view of this attribute, I examine the descriptions of the 'effective communicator' ideal, which are presented in Table 3.5.

The phrases I highlighted in the parallel descriptions indicate what the program designers imagine as part of the desired communicative competence. Variably, it is associated with written and spoken communication, interpersonal skills, use of communication technology and portraying a religious identity.

The recurrent, parallel ideas noted demonstrate the intertextuality of institutional and government documents. The program prospectuses' reference to communication as a desired graduate skill linked to written and

Table 3.4 Placement of 'communication' in program prospectuses for BSA

2007 BSA Program prospectus	2018 BSA Program prospectus
Program specification 1. Program title 2. Name of final award 3. Awarding institution 4. College/school 5. Program accreditor/assessor 6. Goals and objectives of the program 7. Expected learning outcomes 8. Program structure 9. Admission criteria or requirements to the program 10. Other requirements 11. Date the program specifications were written or revised BSA program checklist/flowchart Curriculum map **Expected graduate attributes**	Description Identity **1. Graduate attributes** **2. Accountancy graduate attributes** 3. Philosophy **4. Objectives** **5. Program intended learning outcomes** 6. Program recognitions

Table 3.5 'Effective communicator' as an expected university graduate attribute

2007 BSA Program prospectus	2018 BSA Program prospectus
Effective communicator • Communicates effectively and confidently **in a range of contexts and for many different audiences** • Listens attentively to the intent and spirit of others' words and **responds appropriately verbally and nonverbally** • Composes and comprehends **a range of written, spoken and visual text** to convey information that is meaningful **to society and the Church** • Explores ideas critically and expresses them clearly **for a variety of purposes** • **Uses individual and group performances** to explore and express ideas, thoughts, feelings, and values and understandings	Effective communicator and collaborator • Express myself clearly, correctly and confidently **in various environments, contexts and technologies of human interaction** • **Work productively with individuals or groups** from diverse cultures and demographics • Show profound respect for individual differences and/or uniqueness **as members of God's creation**

spoken expression echoes the government guideline's rhetoric. At the same time, the universities' agency is reflected in new notions of communication articulated in the skills description. Specifically, reference to the relational, technological and religious dimensions of communication potentially reflect some aspect of the schools' institutional habitus (Bourdieu, 1990).

One institutional tendency reflected in these proposed notions of communication is the neoliberal orientation of education to focus on 'the inculcation of skills that make students the sort of flexible entrepreneurial agents best fitted for the contemporary workforce' (Urciuoli, 2010: 52). The addition of social skills and digital literacy in the composition of the ideal communicative graduate stretches the roster of generic skills – those abilities that are broadly applicable and transferable across occupations – that are seen as valuable capital for employment (Blackmore *et al.*, 2017; Smith *et al.*, 2018).

Another institutional disposition reflected in the description of an 'effective communicator' is related to the schools' religious identity. This is indicated by explicit references to religious notions. The absence of these tokens in the government guidelines is to be expected as policy documents apply to all higher education institutions – with or without religious affiliation. In the institutional application of the government framework, however, the program prospectuses of the participant universities make salient the institutions' Catholic identity. This introduces a religious dimension to the communication ideology. More precisely, accountancy graduates of these top-performing schools are expected to communicate in a way that reflects their identity as members of 'the Church' and of 'God's creation'. This implies a religious, moral or ethical standard for communication, which extends the view of an 'effective' communicator. Supported by research identifying religiousness as influencing ethical attitudes and practices of accountants (e.g. Siu *et al.*, 2000; Zarei *et al.*, 2016), this religious conceptualization of communication may be seen as a device to distinguish their accounting graduates on the basis of their ability to communicate not only socially and technologically, but also ethically.

3.3.3 'Communication' at unit level

The program plan described in the BSA prospectus guides the designing of units included in the curriculum. At this level, I examine unit descriptions, which are generally patterned after samples in the government guidelines but are finalized by faculty members designated to teach the specific courses. Repeated close readings of the descriptions reveal which components of the BSA curriculum topicalize 'communication' and related notions (language proficiency, writing, speaking, interpersonal skills, technology and religion), which have been identified from the policy and program documents.

Table 3.6 shows that 'communication' is present in different components of the BSA curriculum. In the 2018 BSA program, courses that belonged to the 2007 business education component were redesigned either as an accounting course or as a professional elective. Professional electives, a new component of the 2018 curriculum, are courses that provide specific training for professional careers. Examples of electives are *Accounting for business combinations*, *Accounting for government and nonprofit organizations* and *English for accountants*. As a feature of courses, communication is variably evidenced in unit descriptions as part of the course title (e.g. *Basic communication and study skills*), as a course topic, as a learning outcome or as a form of assessment.

Table 3.6 Placement of 'communication' in BSA course descriptions

BSA curriculum component	2007 Course descriptions				2018 Course descriptions			
	Title	Topic	Learning outcome	Assessment	Title	Topic	Learning outcome	Assessment
Accounting education	–	1	–	7	–	3	1	11
Business education	1	2	1	4	–	–	–	–
General education	11	9	10	7	3	2	4	4
Professional electives	–	–	–	–	1	3	1	10
Total	12	12	11	18	4	8	6	25

Table 3.7 Notions of communication in BSA course descriptions

Notions of communication	2007 Course descriptions			2018 Course descriptions			
	Accounting education	Business education	General education	Accounting education	Business education	General education	Professional electives
Writing	7	3	11	12	5	10	2
Speaking	4	2	9	6	4	5	1
Interpersonal skills	1	1	–	–	–	1	2
Technology	–	–	–	–	–	1	2
English	–	–	4	–	–	1	1
Filipino	–	–	4	–	2	–	–
Academic context	1	–	6	–	2	–	–
Professional context	1	1	1	3	1	6	2
Accounting field context	1	–	3	1	2	–	1
Diverse/real-life context	–	–	2	–	1	–	–
Religion/ethics	–	–	2	–	1	–	–
National identity	–	–	1	–	1	–	–
Total	15	7	43	22	19	24	11

After examining where 'communication' is positioned in the unit texts, I examined next the notions that are linked to it. Table 3.7 shows the number of times each notion of communication was manually tagged in the course descriptions.

The notions identified in the table indicate that the targeted ability of students to 'effectively' communicate is linked to generic skills (writing, speaking, interpersonal skills, technology), languages (English, Filipino), contexts (academic, professional, accounting, real-life) and identity (religious, national). Collectively, the information in Tables 3.6 and 3.7 indicate three shifts in the way 'communication' is constructed in the unit level – which units teach communication skills, what contexts of communication they are trained for, and what language they use.

First, the positioning of this pedagogical target is seen as extending from general education – the policy-designated province of communication training – to accounting and professional units. The noted saliency of communication outside the 2018 general curriculum may be attributed to the mandatory reduction of general education units at university level as a result of the K to 12 reform. With all language units in the 2007 BSA program devolved to senior high, there are now less units in the 2018 accountancy program explicitly designed for the development of communication skills. At the same time, more reference to communication as part of unit assessments in accounting and professional courses suggests the tendency for the proposed notions of communication to colonize the performance and production of discipline-specific knowledge.

Second, the unit descriptions have moved from targeting communication for academic purposes to emphasizing its professional use. The new emphasis on professional communication is evidence of the economy-driven, instrumental attitude of education that is noted in the Philippine education policies (see Section 3.3.1). This, too, was observed by Blackmore *et al.* (2017) in the context of Australian accounting education. Their findings show that the employment experience of Chinese accounting graduates in Australia highlight the role of university education in 'the production of professional habitus in students by inculcating those dispositions seen to be relevant to the workplace' (Blackmore *et al.*, 2017: 84). Similarly, the entextualized shift in focus from academic to professional communication in the Philippine accounting curriculum foregrounds a neoliberal orientation of education.

Third, in terms of language training, there appears to be more curricular space allocated to Filipino instruction in the new curriculum. Of course, the absence of an explicit English language course in the 2018 general curriculum does not necessarily indicate a deprioritization of English. Indeed, the importance of English is deeply entrenched in policies for program design (see Section 3.3.1) and is, in fact, the predominant language of curricular rhetoric. That is, it is the language for the presentation of the curriculum except for the descriptions of the two new Filipino language units.

> *Filipino 1 Kontekstuwalisadong Komunikasyon sa Filipino*
>
> *Ang Kontekstuwalisadong Komunikasyon sa Filipino ay isang kursong pangwika na lilinang sa kasanayan ng mga mag-aaral sa kolehiyo sa mahusay na pagdidiskurso sa anyong pasalita at pasulat, gayundin sa pananaliksik, salig sa disiplina ng akawntansi, komersiyo, at pangasiwaang pangnegosyo gamit ang wikang Filipino. Saklaw ng kurso ang pagsusuri sa gampanin ng Filipino sa pagpapaunlad ng sarili at ng bansa, ang kritikal na pagbasa bilang susi sa pag-unawa ng mga tekstong*

akademiko at propesyonal, ang pagtuklas at paglinang ng mga kaalaman batay sa mga lokal o katutubong konteksto, ang pagsusuri sa katayuan ng Filipino sa mga piling larangan, at ang gamit ng Filipino sa mismong disiplinang kinabibilangan. Layunin din ng kurso na maitaas ang kamalayang global ng mga mag-aaral upang makapag-ambag sa kanilang sariling pag-unlad habang pinalalalim ang makaPilipino at maka-[UniB] pagpapahalaga na may pagtangkilik sa sariling pagkakakilanlan at kultura. Sa pagtatapos ng kurso, inaasahang maipamamalas ng mga mag-aaral ang kakayahan sa mabisang paggamit ng Filipino sa mga diskursong akademiko at propesyonal sa larangan ng akawntansi, komersiyo, pananaiksik at pangasiwaang pangnegosyo tungo sa intelektuwalisasyon ng wikang pambansa.

[Filipino 1 Contextualized Communication in Filipino

Contextualized Communication in Filipino is a language course that develops college students' skills in effective spoken and written discourse, as well as in doing research in accounting, commerce, and business using the Filipino language. The course examines the role of Filipino in developing the self and the nation, critical reading as key to understanding academic and professional texts, the discovery and enhancement of local and indigenous knowledge, and the status of Filipino in selected fields, particularly its use in the discipline to which the students belong. The course also aims to raise students' global awareness to contribute to their self-development while deepening Filipino and [institutional] values that promote their self-identity and culture. At the end of the course, students are expected to demonstrate proficient use of Filipino in academic and professional discourse in accounting, commerce, research, and business toward the intellectualization of the national language.]

Filipino 2 Panimulang Pagsasalin sa Filipino

Layunin ng kurso na mapahalagahan ang ugnayan ng mga wika sa loob at labas ng bansa at ang kakayahan ng wikang Filipino bilang intelektuwalisadong wika. Sa gayon malilinang ang kamalayang global ng mga mag-aaral na nakaangkla sa paguugnay ng mga wika at kultura. Nakapokus ang Panimulang Pagsasalin sa Filipino sa mga batayang kaalaman at konsepto sa pagsasalin sa Filipino bilang tunguhang wika. Tatalakayin dito ang mga simulain, proseso at prinsipyo sa pagsasalin upang mahubog ang mas malalim na pag-unawa at mabisang paggamit ng wikang Filipino kaugnay ng tinatahak na akademikong disiplina. Matapos ang kurso, ang mga mag-aaral ay inaasahang: natatalakay ang mga batayang konsepto tungkol sa kalikasan, katangian, proseso at mga prinsipyo ng pagsasalin bilang gawaing pangwika; naipaliliwanag ang pangunahing simulain, usapin at hamon sa pagsasalin sa Filipino; natutukoy ang mga katangiang dapat taglayin ng epektibong tagasalin sa Filipino; nakasusuri ng mga halimbawang saling pampubliko at popular; nakapagsasalin ng mga tekstong disiplinal; nakapagsusulat ng mapanuri at lohikal na teksto na taglay ang pag-unawa sa mga kahingian ng pagsasalin sa sariling disiplina; at naipamamalas ang

> *maka-[UniB] pagpapahalaga sa pagsasagawa ng mga gawaing kaugnay sa kurso.*
>
> [Filipino 2 Introduction to Translation in Filipino
>
> The course seeks to promote the relationship between languages within and beyond the country and the distinction of Filipino as an intellectualized language. In this way, students' global awareness will be developed anchored in the connection of language and culture. Introduction to Translation in Filipino is focused on basic knowledge and concepts in translation with Filipino as target language. To be discussed are the fundamentals, process, and principles of translation in order to form and deepen understanding and proficient use of the Filipino language in the specific academic discipline. At the end of the course, students are expected to be able to: discuss the basic concepts of the nature, qualities, process, and principles of translation as language work; explain the fundamentals, issues, and challenges of translation in Filipino; identify the qualities of an effective translator in Filipino; evaluate examples of public and popular translations; translate disciplinal texts; write critical and logical texts that display understanding of the demands of translation in the specific discipline; and demonstrate [institutional] valuing of course work.]

Both Filipino 1 and 2 resulted from the widely media-covered campaign of a group of educators (mostly Filipino language teachers) to retain Filipino courses in the 2018 general curriculum on grounds that the removal of Filipino units in higher education is an unconstitutional, 'anti-Filipino' move (Claudio, 2014: n.p.). The lobbying group justified this position by citing Article 6 of the 1987 Constitution:

> The national language of the Philippines is Filipino. As it evolves, it shall be further developed and enriched on the basis of existing Philippine and other languages. Subject to provisions of law and as the Congress may deem appropriate, the Government shall take steps to initiate and sustain the use of Filipino as medium of official communication and as language of instruction in the educational system.

The proposed logic is that removing Filipino language units from the university curriculum will effectively limit its use as medium of education, which is then viewed as a strategic 'attack against the national language' (Geronimo, 2014: n.p.). As a counterproposition, the group called for the creation of Filipino language units that, as reflected in the unit descriptions, construct Filipino as a language of intellectual discourse, as a legitimate language for academic and professional communication, and as an index of personal, institutional and national identity and progress.

Overall, the description of units included in the BSA curriculum indicate that the rhetoric on communication is extending beyond general education, beyond academic use and beyond English proficiency. Having examined the position and notions of communication in curricular rhetoric, I now turn to a more focused analysis of the effective communication ideal constructed in the corpus.

3.4 The Construction of 'Effective Communication'

To achieve a more fine-grained understanding of what constitutes 'effectiveness' of communication from the view of accounting education decision makers, I used the AntConc (Anthony, 2019) collocates, cluster and concordance tools. This quantitative approach bears out language patterns that are statistically significant and potentially relevant indicators of dominant ideologies held by accounting education authorities. Key lexical results were then connected to the notions identified in the first phase of the corpus analysis to gain a sense of the valuing of specific communicative abilities in the training of future accountants.

To determine significant collocates, the collocate frequency was set to a minimum of 5, as recommended by the software developer. Using this standard, I began with the key search terms: 'communicate' and 'communication'. Table 3.8 shows the top lexical collocates.

The results validate the frequent pairing of 'effective communication' and 'communicate effectively/effectively communicate'. This patterned use of the modifier reinforces the need to clarify the evaluative concept of effectiveness. To do this, I examine in turn the lexical collocates of 'communication' in order of statistical significance.

Table 3.8 Top collocates of 'communicate' and 'communication'

Search term	Rank	Statistical strength of collocate	Collocate
communicate	1	11.45349	effectively
communication	1	9.35395	interpersonal
	2	7.61698	skills
	3	7.53681	managing
	4	7.53292	effective
	6	7.30664	technical
	7	7.16632	personal
	8	7.10602	technology
	9	7.03202	communication
	10	6.57634	part

3.4.1 Communicating relationships

The strongest collocate of communication is 'interpersonal'. This term was found to frequently co-occur with words such as 'communication', 'skills' and 'management'. Probing these patterns, the concordance shows that these collocations regularly refer to 'nonprofessional knowledge', 'conflict management', 'organizational management' and 'teamwork'. This usage pattern reflects an understanding of interpersonal competence as the ability to communicate in a way that facilitates cooperation and resolves tensions between and among members of a group. In other words, it is the ability to communicate for relational goals.

The emphasis given to this type of communication in the corpus is consistent with literature on employability skills that identifies interpersonal ability as a generic or soft skill that is relevant across occupations and professional ranks (e.g. Boyle *et al.*, 2014; Spence & Carter, 2014). The premium placed by the curriculum on developing interpersonal ability can be traced back to the neoliberal goal of (re)producing skills that can potentially increase the marketability of graduates. Indeed, the ability to work well in teams is among the 'generic dispositions associated with employability' (Blackmore *et al.*, 2017: 76).

However, the specific interest of the BSA program in targeting students' social skills may also be linked to issues raised concerning accounting majors' purported shyness or introversion (e.g. Granleese & Barrett, 1990; Simons *et al.*, 1995). The emphasis in the corpus on this social aspect of communication is possibly a reaction to reports on the perceived relational skills deficit of accounting students, which feeds into the 'poor communicator' stereotype of accountants (see Chapter 1). However, what constitutes 'good' interpersonal communication is not further elaborated in the curricular documents. Understanding this notion entails examining interactions in the classroom (see Chapter 4) and in the office (see Part 2) where social actors differentially perform teamwork through linguistic choices and discursive construction of rapport and trust.

Next to interpersonal skills, the second highest collocate of 'communication' in the corpus is 'skills'. The concordance suggests a link between 'communication skills' and four other recurrent contexts of usage: (1) writing, (2) speaking, (3) communication technology and (4) language proficiency. I now examine each of these types of 'communication skills' in turn.

3.4.2 Written communication

Writing as a communication skill is made salient by diverse references to genres (memos, essays, proposals), text types (descriptive, formal), other language skills or tasks (reading, speaking) and an evaluative standard (coherent). The forms of writing highlighted in the corpus represent genres that are academic and professional. That 'essay/s' are among the top collocates of 'writing' however indicates greater attention to developing students' academic writing skills.

This pattern suggests the importance of literacy in higher education, confirming its status as a 'tool of power' in this domain (Piller, 2017b). While there is this indication of focus on writing for academic purposes, there is also the expectation that the skill is transferable to the work domain, for instance, enabling graduates to compose business memos and proposals. The expectation that this generic skill is produced in universities for application in the profession is foregrounded in accounting research investigating employers' feedback on accounting graduates writing skills (e.g. Andrews & Koester, 1973), emphasizing the value of writing in accounting practice (Nellermoe *et al.*, 1999; Tenedero & Vizconde, 2015), and calling for more curricular attention to this 'neglected skill' (Andrews & Sigband, 1984: 20). Indeed, writing skills are a salient part of the 'skills gap' discourse in accounting literature, influencing professional policy, such as the move to assess writing skills in the CPA licensure exam (VanZante & Person, 1994).

Potentially contributing to this concern over graduates' literacy skills are new demands in globalized employment. In the offshoring sector, for example, outsourced roles typically involve routine work such as data encoding and record management. These kinds of back-office tasks are seen as putting 'more pressure on literacy skills' (Cameron, 2002: 72). At curricular level, it remains vague what notions of literacy exactly are valued in various accounting positions. What kinds of literacy practices are valued in the workplace only becomes apparent with reference to practitioner knowledge (see Section 4.5.1) and ritualized written assessments for corporate employment (see Section 5.4).

3.4.3 Spoken communication

Strongly correlated with writing, speaking is the other productive skill typically linked to communication. Unsurprisingly, speaking and writing are frequently targeted together. Compared with writing, however, there are notably fewer collocates for 'speaking', suggesting less attention to developing students' oral expression. The tendency to undervalue oral communication training has been linked to lack of understanding of the real nature of accounting work (Ameen, Bruns *et al.*, 2010). Employer-informed studies report speaking as a core function in accounting practice (Albrecht & Sack, 2000; Miller & Stone, 2009).

Students' expectation (construed as a misconception) that accounting work only minimally involves public speaking has been identified as part of the attraction of this career to introverts, who generally prefer quiet, individual work to audience-facing, speaking roles (Ameen, Jackson *et al.*, 2010). This proposed connection between introversion and the imagined minimally vocal work of accountants relates to the typecasting of accountants as 'poor communicators' vis-à-vis the extrovert ideal. As Cain (2012) argued, we live in a world that tends to see extroverts as better communicators. This deficit view of introverts is further validated by claims about accounting students being more speech anxious than their peers in other disciplines (Hassall *et al.*, 2000). Consequently, action research has taken to monitoring and managing students' communication apprehension levels (Gardner *et al.*, 2005; Miller & Stone, 2009) and developing their speech skills for accountant–client interactions (e.g. Burns & Moore, 2007).

Set against this backdrop of literature, oracy as a target communication skill remains ambiguous in Philippine curricular rhetoric. This may be seen negatively as reflecting a limitation or an imbalance in the curriculum that appears to be more focused on literacy. The absence of prescribed notions of 'speaking', however, provides room for agency in instruction, enabling teachers to deploy differential advice or guidance on 'good' speaking habits or 'effective' speech both for pedagogical (see Sections 4.2 to 4.5) and employment purposes (see Section 5.3). At the same time, the vagueness of the desired speaking competence indicates that effective speech is an abstraction. This foregrounds the point that what counts as effective communication is, indeed, culture- and context-specific. Outside these social parameters, one can only speak of notions in generalities.

3.4.4 Communicating through technology

'Communication skills' is also markedly used in contexts where 'technology' is mentioned. This suggests that effective communication in the view of accounting education authorities involves knowledge and skill in relevant forms of technology that facilitate communication. The relevance of this conceptual correlation is further qualified by the cluster test that determines significant language patterns across the entire corpus. The only resultant lexical pairing indicated in the concordance is 'communication technology'. This phrase is the only highly frequent lexical pairing across the entire corpus, which suggests a strong connection between the targeted communication competence and technological literacy.

'Technology' is most frequently used with 'science', 'information', 'communication', 'role', 'knowledge', 'using', 'business' and 'management'. These collocation patterns foreground the role of technology in the production of knowledge – especially scientific or technical (such as business or management information) – as well as in communicating such knowledge. The connection between technology and knowledge production and performance suggests the priority of keeping up to date with technical proficiencies necessary to navigate computer-mediated communication. Besides requiring instrumental competence with digital tools, technologization is also creating new genres (Fairclough, 2003) and reshaping discursive practices (Iedema & Wodak, 1999). These changes have the effect of shifting the value of communication from embodied forms, such as face-to-face conversations, to digital forms (Gist-Mackey, 2018). This in turn calls for extending the scope of literacy training in university to include technological literacy, including the strategic use of multimodal features of online software (García, 2014) for high-stakes communication events such as the job interview video call (Dadas, 2018).

Overall, the curricular rhetoric seems to be grounded in a general recognition of the increasingly important role of technology in the new economy. The salience of technology in globalized, transnational work heightens the desirability of graduates who can perform their skills – including speaking and writing – through various digital channels for recruitment and work purposes (more on this in Part 2).

3.4.5 Communicating in English and Filipino

In terms of languages, communication skills in the accounting curriculum are linked to English and Filipino. The lexical collocates of English are 'language', 'program' and 'course' while the top collocates of 'Filipino' are '*gamit* [use]', '*wikang* [language]' and 'literature'.

The concordance for the lexical collocates of 'English' reveal that the majority of the tokens occur in the 2007 documents. Frequent mentions of 'English' in the old curriculum reflects the priority of developing students' competence in English as the language of business. These references emphasize English proficiency as a prerequisite for admission to the BSA program and for success in the global workplace. In the 2018 curriculum, 'English' also figures in the description of an elective course, which emphasizes its value as the medium of communication in accounting firms. It appears then that explicit references to 'English' highlight its significance as a linguistic capital that students must both already possess and still enhance in order to pass as both academically and professionally competent. This view of English as the language of accounting is further entrenched through its use as the medium of the curriculum, demonstrating that the economic order functions as a 'covert form of language policy, which imposes English as a natural and neutral medium of academic excellence' (Piller & Cho, 2013: 24).

Alongside English, the value of Filipino is articulated in the new curriculum on the basis of its academic and disciplinal instrumentality. The Filipino language units included in the 2018 general curriculum asserts the national language as a pedagogical priority supported by rhetoric of national pride. The symbolic equivalence of the Filipino language to patriotism, however, has been discredited in surveys examining Filipinos' views of the national language and of English (Sibayan & Gonzalez, 1996). But no matter what perception studies report, this ideology continues to be deployed in government and education rhetoric so that, for instance, removing Filipino language units from higher education is castigated by lobbyists as 'anti-Filipino' (Claudio, 2014: n.p.). Interestingly, when this argument won, the advocates designed language units that propose an enlarged view of Filipino as linguistic capital not only for national identification but also for global participation. This new rhetoric may be viewed as a strategy to expand the symbolic status of Filipino by positioning it as a legitimate language of the global new economy, particularly as its actual value in the globalized accounting workplace is easily lost in the shadow of English hegemony. This is similar to Urla's (2012) report on the Basque language revival movement in Spain where language advocates used the logics of markets and entrepreneurialism to re-affirm the value of minoritized languages beyond cultural identification.

Overall, the curricular rhetoric positions English and Filipino alongside each other as languages of academic and professional discourse. The dynamics of bilingualism, however, is, of course, much more nuanced as social actors variably deploy their linguistic repertoire in situational interactions in the classroom (see Chapter 4) and at work (more on this in Part 2).

3.4.6 Communicating in context

Finally, 'communication' is also linked to contexts ('managing', 'technical', 'personal') where the competence may be applied. The analysis of unit descriptions earlier identified four common sites of communication: academia, profession, field and real life (see Table 3.7). I used these search terms to probe curricular ideas about contextualized communication. Exploring the concordance lines for the top collocates of each search term reveals that general education and content courses focus on different contexts for the application of students' knowledge and skills. For instance, the top collocates for 'academic' (i.e. 'reading', 'writing', 'faculty' and 'skills') are all found in general education course descriptions – particularly for language classes. Meanwhile, the collocates of 'field' (i.e. 'accountancy' and 'business'), 'profession' (i.e. 'public', 'accountancy' and 'accounting') and 'real life' (i.e. 'cases', 'life' and 'problems') significantly figure in texts related to accounting and business courses. This observation indicates that general education is mainly concerned with developing students' academic literacy to meet specific course targets and to transfer these skills in other contexts within academia, such as in accounting and business classes (Lea & Street, 1998). In contrast, content courses, which students often refer to as their 'major' classes, prioritize the development of their disciplinal literacy, that is, their 'ability to appropriately participate in the communicative practices of a discipline' (Airey, 2011: 3), in this case, accounting and business.

The rhetorical designation of curriculum components to particular sites for the performance of communicative competence is captured in Airey's (2011) model of disciplinary literacy, which identifies three sites where students' skills are enacted: the academy, society and the workplace.

The dominant rhetoric of general courses is to equip students to communicate in school. Meanwhile, content courses tend to focus on the ability to communicate in wider society and the workplace, which are constructed as constituting 'real life'. This seemingly positivist observation suggests that the reduction of general education classes in the 2018 curriculum signals an increase in the priority of developing disciplinary literacy in accounting practice, which is linked to the aim of making graduates more competitive in the professional field. On the other hand, it also hints at the marginalization of general education training which, like liberal arts education, is not strongly oriented toward training students for particular jobs (Urciuoli, 2014).

This interpretation foregrounds the neoliberal tendency of higher education to shape the curriculum according to standards of the new economy. It also suggests a polarity in the knowledge represented by academic teachers in general education and practitioner teachers who convene content and professional units (see Section 4.5). The distinction made between academic and 'real-life' situations likewise indicates an expectation that communication training and practices in school and at work differ (more on this in Part 2).

3.5 Summary

This chapter has explored the ideational function of education documents with regard to 'communication'. While existing studies on the communication training of accountants has largely relied on survey methods to identify what teachers and students consider as indicators of the ideal communicative competence, I have demonstrated the use of discourse analysis through corpus methods as an alternative approach to exploring language ideologies of social actors as reflected in documents authored by them. Highlighting where 'communication' is positioned in the curriculum and what notions are frequently paired with it, this analysis contributes new understandings of how social actors at the top of the accounting education structure differentially construct communication as part of students' preparation for accounting practice. The findings also demonstrate the fluidity of the rhetoric of 'good' communication, shifting over time between monolingualism and bilingualism and between academic and professional contexts, as shown in Figure 3.1.

While more varied notions of communication have been gleaned from the corpus, Figure 3.1 synthesizes the conceptualizations that are statistically significant. Iterations in the different document types are indicated by boxes. The more boxed a particular notion, the more entrenched it is in the curricular rhetoric on communication. Focusing on these intersections shows that generic skills (speaking and writing, interpersonal skills, technological competence) are the most saliently reproduced notions of the desired communicative ability. This

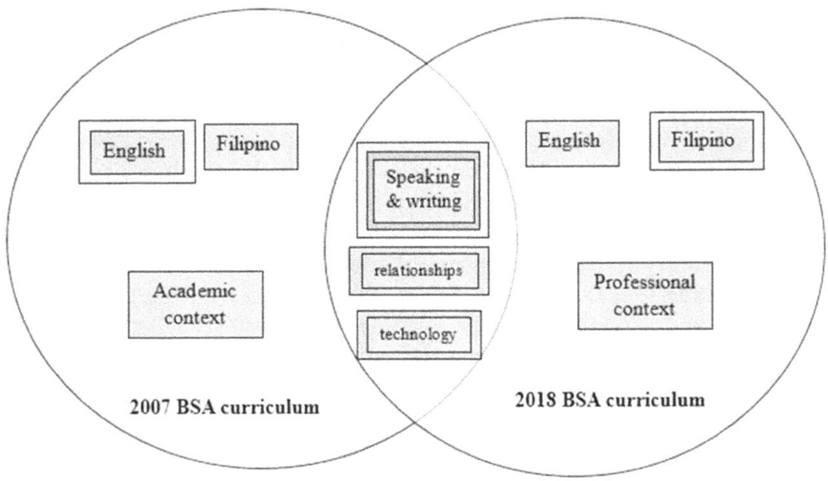

Figure 3.1 Dominant notions of communication in accounting education documents

recurrence suggests the strong and consistent valuing of skills that are broadly useful in globalized workplaces across a major educational reform.

Also telling are the points of divergence across the two periods in curriculum development. Variation in the linguistic and contextual notions of communication in the 2007 and 2018 BSA curricula indicates shifts in the value given to developing students' academic and professional literacies in English and Filipino. Whereas English is firmly positioned as the language of academic and professional success, Filipino is discursively positioned alongside it as a language of intellectual discourse in the same domains, on institutional, national and global scales. Accompanying this shift are rhetorical suggestions – particularly in media reports about the retention of Filipino language units in the new curriculum – that these two official languages are competing for recognition as capital for the performance of identity and competence. Whether and how this idea is taken up in actual communication instruction is part of the analysis in the next chapter.

The desire to produce graduates who can communicate effectively in these widely varied contexts – in line with their present academic and future professional goals, in both the national and global arenas – makes decisions about communication training complicated. This observation echoes Kuteeva and Airey's (2014: 534) point that in countries where academic literacy is developed in and through two or more languages – in the Philippine case, English and Filipino – 'the balance between these disciplinal languages is contested and intimately related to the acquisition of disciplinary knowledge'. To probe how these tensions are shaped and negotiated, it is necessary to examine how these entextualized ideologies are enacted. This is what we turn to in the next chapter, which focuses on how teachers and students co-shape communication training in the classroom.

4 Communicating in the Accounting Classroom

4.1 Introduction

This chapter extends the inquiry into the language practices and ideologies in accounting education, by examining how communication is done in classes attended by accounting students. Focusing on how teachers and students use, view and value language in the classroom, this analysis builds on the findings of the previous chapter, which examined how 'effective communication' is constructed in curricular documents produced by social actors at the top of the accounting education structure. The findings showed that this target learning outcome is variably constructed in curricular rhetoric in terms of productive skills (literacy, oracy), linguistic code (English, Filipino), related literacies (interpersonal, technology) and context (academic, professional). With these conceptualizations of the desired communicative competence as a reference point, I now explore through observation and interview data how the notions of communication are conveyed, interpreted, enacted, challenged and negotiated in classroom interactions of teachers and students – social actors at the other end of the field hierarchy. To this end, I discuss four aspects of communication that emerged from school-based ethnographic data: the use of English and Filipino as teaching languages (Section 4.2), practices of both teachers and students in communicating knowledge (Section 4.3), relationships (Section 4.4) and signs of communicative competence in the workplace (Section 4.5), as well as ideologies undergirding these practices.

4.2 The 'Superstar' and 'Sidekick' Language of Instruction

Language is central to education. It is the primary means through which teachers communicate knowledge to students and through which students, in turn, demonstrate the knowledge they have acquired in the process.

In the absence of an explicit institutional language policy, teachers in accounting schools are free to determine what language is appropriate for use in classroom instruction. Hence, they assume the role of primary language agents in charge of constructing and implementing classroom-level language policy (Henderson, 2017). What policy they construct and enforce is differentially shaped by their beliefs about languages and the very nature of the subject they teach as either language-focused or content-focused.

4.2.1 Language use in language classes

In language classes, typically, the mandatory medium is the target language indexed in the course title. This linguistic code is featured in two ways – as content and as medium of instruction. This dual emphasis on language serves as a pretext for monolingual policy, like the English-only policy (EOP) in Ms Aurora's English language unit:

Excerpt 4.1

Ms Aurora: I use English in teaching. (…) When the students speak to me or when they do group discussions in the class, I make sure that they use English. (…) It is an unwritten policy in my class to communicate in English. I do this to make them comfortable with using the language.

The policy of using only English is justified by the pedagogical priority of the class, which is to improve students' competence in the language of focus. That the EOP is 'unwritten' suggests that it is silently understood, its normalcy implied and unquestioned. This sense of normalcy is potentially internalized by the students through the explicit management by the language teacher who 'make[s] sure they use English' and the teacher's own monolingual practice in teaching. Hence, the nature of the course and the teacher's language management and modeling contribute to normalizing monolingual policy. This unquestioned practice reflects the view of languages as separate and distinct (Henderson, 2017), each one a closed system that is believed to be learned best when used exclusively.

However, this same logic does not operate in the case of a Filipino language class I observed, where the use of the featured language (Filipino) appears to be more preferential than prescriptive. This is evident in Ms Edna's recount of her Filipino language class with students, who, coming from international high schools, were reportedly more fluent in English than Filipino.

Excerpt 4.2

Ms Edna: …*karamihan talaga sila mga* English speaking. So *talagang nung una medyo* disappointed *ako kasi ayaw mag-recite. Yun pala kasi natatakot sila magsalita kasi hindi sila magaling mag-Tagalog. Kasi in-e-expect na pag Filipino ka nag-ta-Tagalog. Pero in-encourage ko sila--Sige, sige mag-Taglish kayo basta i-express nyo lang yung* thoughts *ninyo. Yun! Marami na nag-re-recite* then eventually *nasasanay na rin sila na*

> *siyempre naririnig nila ako nagta-Tagalog so nagta-Tagalog na rin sila kahit medyo pashwar-shwar-shwar ang Tagalog nila.*
>
> [...most of them are really English speaking. So, really, in the beginning I was a bit disappointed because they did not want to recite. Then I found out they're afraid to talk because they don't speak Tagalog well. Because it's expected that if the subject is Filipino then we speak Tagalog. But I encouraged them--Go ahead, speak Taglish, express your thoughts. There! Many began to recite, then eventually they got used to it because, of course, they hear me speak in Tagalog so they speak in Tagalog also, even if they speak Tagalog with an English accent.]

In contrast to the strict monolingualism enforced by Ms Aurora in her English class, Ms Edna allows bilingualism in her Filipino class, which takes the form of Taglish or Tagalog-English code switching. On one hand, the sanctioned use of Taglish may be seen as a teaching strategy to manage students' plurilingual or unequal proficiencies in the languages available in their repertoire (Leung & Valdés, 2019; Tamtomo, 2018), which Bautista (2004: 227) calls 'deficiency-driven code-switching'. On the other hand, as this practice is allowed in a context that is typically linked to monolingual Filipino, the accommodation of English indicates an ideological hierarchization of languages. That certain languages or varieties (such as Taglish) are allowed in particular contexts (here, a Filipino language class) emphasizes the potential of language to represent not only a valued form of knowledge (sociocultural capital) but also an index of social status and prestige (symbolic capital) (Bourdieu, as cited in Watts, 2011).

The ascription of status to languages is very salient in the Philippine context, as documented in studies that link varieties of English and Tagalog spoken by Filipinos to the socioeconomic class and education levels of their speakers. Specifically, monolingual English (especially based on native standard forms such as American English) and Taglish (especially with American English accent) are associated with the highly educated, private-schooled, upper-middle class who hold positions of influence in politics, education or media (Bautista, 1996; Sibayan & Gonzalez, 1996). In contrast, Taglish (with regional accent) and monolingual Tagalog are linked to lower-class job placements such as nannies (Bautista, 1982) and factory workers (Go & Gustilo, 2013). Such explicit linking of languages to the socioeconomic order reifies the status of English (Piller & Cho, 2013) and, by extension, Taglish (with American English accent) as 'language for the elite' (Ricento, 2018: 6).

This legitimization of Taglish in a Filipino class is additionally supported by another contention of Ms Edna: '*Parang hindi na uso yung "Taglish" na salita kasi ganito tayo mag-communicate e. Filipino siya.* [The label "Taglish" is practically outmoded because this is really how we communicate. It's Filipino.]' This statement reflects a different stance toward bilingualism in English and Filipino, which echoes the argument that owing to its widespread use, Taglish is considered the lingua franca or the *de facto* national language, bearing features of both standard English and standard Tagalog (Bautista, 2004). Arguing for this equivalence (Taglish = Filipino) has the effect of erasing the distinction between accent-based varieties of Taglish that differentially index membership in upper-middle and lower class. This view of Taglish then shifts the focus from Taglish as an index of limited Tagalog proficiency (Excerpt 4.2) to Taglish as a legitimate form of the course's target language. By implication, this alternative view renders the supposed deficient form (Taglish) acceptable in a Filipino language class.

In sum, medium of instruction is straightforward in English language classes, where monolingual bias for English is the norm. Language choice in Filipino language classes, however, is more complex. While monolingual practice is a recognized norm, it does not necessarily prevail, as ideologies about the status of English, Filipino and Taglish (as well as views about Taglish as an index of limited proficiency in Filipino or as a legitimate form of Filipino) shape decisions about which languages and varieties are allowed in classroom discourse.

4.2.2 Language use in content classes

In classes where language acquisition is not the main objective of the course, that is accounting and business classes (also referred to as content classes), the language that is legitimized for classroom use also varies, relative to individual teachers' language ideologies. In one accounting class, the teacher (Mr Basilio) made the exclusive use of English a class policy.

Excerpt 4.3

Mr Basilio: (...) when I teach, well, we actually speak in English. I require my students to speak in English because I know that in the workplace English is actually needed. Okay, because I actually work in an accounting firm. Well, of course in our work, well, we have clients who are actually foreigners, so in that case you have to speak in English. (...) So that's why in my class, somehow I am training them in their oral communication because they have to do presentations. (...) it's also a practice when they do presentation *kasi* [because] in work, well, you have to present, for example, in front of a client.

Mr Basilio justifies implementing EOP by referring to the currency of the language in the accounting firm where he is a partner. In describing actual workplace scenarios where English is valued, he elevates the status of the language as an important part of accounting students' preparation for their target profession. This rhetoric articulates the ideology that English is highly important because it is necessary for employment. It is the language that allows access to quality jobs – such as the one he currently holds – and has great potential to accrue economic and social capital particularly in international work environments (Dumanig *et al.*, 2012; Henderson, 2017; Kuteeva & Airey, 2014), where one collaborates with 'foreigners'. This valuing of English tied to the imagining of students' future professional experiences is a recurring ideology articulated by teachers and also reflected in curricular rhetoric (as discussed in Chapter 3). The academic (re)production of English as priority medium of accounting work will be further examined in Section 4.5.

That English is an important language in globalized accounting work is not contentious. It is, in fact, highly valued and is a popular lingua franca in intercultural work and school contexts. What is problematic, however, is the tendency for schools, through teachers' rhetoric and methods, to equate competence in English with financial success. This widely disseminated 'economic benefit myth' (Parba, 2018; Watts, 2011) has been questioned in critical studies highlighting race, accent and other factors that determine whether, indeed, a worker's English proficiency is rewarded (e.g. Flores & Rosa, 2015; Lippi-Green, 2012). Although this reality is not part of accounting teachers' classroom rhetoric, some of them recognize the merits of not imposing monolingual English.

Excerpt 4.4

Researcher: What do you think is the role of English in accounting education?

Mr Fernando: Larger than life. *O di ba?* [Isn't it?] *Eh di ba siyempre nga* [Isn't it, of course], globalization, internationalization, even if I explain to them in Tagalog, in real life *naman talaga, may mga* [there really are] foreign investors, foreign clients *na kailangan may* [who need] English. So very important.

(...)

Researcher: Do you have a language policy?

Mr Fernando: *Wala naman. Ang hirap eh kasi ako, hindi naman ako* straight English *tapus i-re-require mo so kumbaga para ano lang* (...)[None. It's difficult because I can't speak in straight English myself then if I require that of my students, it's like (...)]

Excerpt 4.5

Researcher: Is English required in your classes?

Ms Diwata: I encourage students.

Researcher: The word is 'encourage'. So it's not mandatory to speak in English all the time?

Ms Diwata: *Eh minsan kasi nawawala sila e.* [The thing is sometimes they are at a loss.]

Excerpt 4.6

Mr Carlo: It's just that I have a rule. If you speak Filipino, you have to be speaking in Filipino straight. If you speak in English, you have to speak, but of course these students they would mix them up. I'm just very forgiving for that. What I'm concerned *lang* [only] is this: that the idea is preserved. If you understand accounting using English, so be it. If it's in Filipino, so be it.

In Excerpt 4.4, the teacher recognizes English as a prestige language, one that is 'larger than life', and a language that students 'need to' speak in class potentially as preparation for workplace encounters with 'foreign investors, foreign clients'. At the same time, Mr Fernando and Ms Diwata (Excerpt 4.5) recognize the reality of limited competence in the language, which encumbers teacher modeling and student display of 'straight English' or the idealized monolingual performance of English. The gap in the linguistic repertoire of teacher and students is bridged by allowing language mixing or shifting to another language in which they can better express themselves, in this case, Filipino (more precisely, Taglish). In Excerpt 4.6, Mr Carlo likewise acknowledges the tendency of students to translanguage or switch from one language to another in their verbal expressions. Along with this, he articulates the dual monolingual norm, which frowns on language mixing and esteems communicating in 'straight English' and 'straight Filipino', typically idealized in language classes (see Section 4.2.1). In these three excerpts, two learning priorities intersect: (1) preparing students to be competitive participants in their future global workplaces by equipping them with the highly valued linguistic capital that is English; and (2) enabling students to meet present learning needs by allowing language variation (through dual monolingualism or codeswitching).

The flexibility of language mixing is linked to effective content learning, which is the more immediate priority of content classes. Accounting students echo this sentiment. For example, final-year accounting student Isko admitted that his low confidence in English makes him hesitant to participate in class. He also disclosed that he is afraid when the professor pushes them to use English only. This problem, which is ignored by EOP advocates, is emphatically critiqued by Kriselda.

Excerpt 4.7

Kriselda: Here in the Philippines, there's this idea that when you use English it's like the best, like number one language of sort. But the thing is *kasi* [because] some students aren't good in English. And as a teacher, as an educator, you should know *na* [that] one language doesn't fit all!

This mirrors the findings of Tamtomo (2018) in vocational schools where teachers allow language variation to manage gaps in the linguistic repertoire of both students and teachers, thereby prioritizing skills transference over language training. While accounting teachers generally align with this practice, they also expressed another priority that tends to rival the aim of delivering accounting knowledge, namely, to prepare students to communicate in their target profession, which is consistently imagined as an English-speaking domain. As evidenced by their rationalization of language practices in class, content teachers contend with targeting two important pedagogical goals: (1) acquiring technical knowledge here and now through bilingual practice and (2) displaying future professionalism or global communicative competence through monolingual English.

In this section, I presented dominant language ideologies communicated by teachers through language policy and language attitude. In an English language class, the monolingual bias is supported by the nature of the unit that targets the specific language and the teacher's linguistic habitus that disposes her to require the exclusive use of the targeted language. However, in a Filipino class, the teacher negotiated the monolingual norm by rationalizing the legitimacy of the codeswitched form of the target language (Taglish), indicating ideologies of linguistic hierarchy. Likewise, language choice is not always clear-cut in content courses, where teachers contend with the twofold task of (1) extending students' fluency practice in English by requiring or encouraging its use in class talk; and (2) attaining current educational objectives by allowing bilingual expression. The reality of unequal competencies in English and Filipino further contributes to the tension between prioritizing English improvement and knowledge acquisition. As course managers, teachers decide whether to let English drive the content exchange in class or to use students' and their own linguistic repertoire as flexible instruments of knowledge. How teachers and students communicate specialized accounting knowledge in class is examined next.

4.3 Communicating Knowledge

Acquiring knowledge of the accounting field is the main aim of the accounting degree program. This knowledge is represented through numbers (e.g. financial statements) and language (e.g. oral presentation of the financial statements). Learning how to analyze, treat and present numbers is central to accounting and business pedagogy. To achieve this pedagogical aim, teachers make decisions about how to communicate specialized knowledge, which includes choosing what language to use in presenting topics to students and in assessing their comprehension or knowledge acquisition.

Traditionally seen as the main source of knowledge in the classroom, teachers strategize to deliver instruction in a way that students can easily understand, and thus successfully transfer the skills targeted in the course. What lecturing language they use is shaped primarily by their language ideologies (see Section 4.2), articulated explicitly through policy and implicitly through their attitude toward classroom communication practices.

While EOP is not common in content classes (only one of six teachers reported having this policy), language practices in class indicate preference for its use in knowledge presentation. In fact, all content teachers lectured first and foremost in English, indexing English as the default language in teacher presentation of knowledge. Ms Helena (business teacher) and Mr Gregorio (accounting teacher) explain the reason for this practice.

Excerpt 4.8

Ms Helena: *Nag-e-English ako depende dun sa* guide *na ginagamit ko* for teaching. So let's say, *ang* PowerPoint *kasi* provided *na*. Provided *ng* publisher. So most of the lectures *siyempre na-prepare na* in English so *dun ako gumagamit ng* English. [I speak in English depending on the guide I use for teaching. So let's say, the PowerPoint is already provided by the publisher. Most of the lectures are already prepared in English so I use English.]

Excerpt 4.9

Mr Gregorio*: Dapat ma'am kasi ano eh* since *yung* subject is in English *dapat* English *din muna yung* interpretation *ma'am kasi* they're dealing with theories in English, *kasama sa* board exam. Even the English subject is *kasama siya sa* board exam ma'am *eh*. [It's a must, ma'am. Since the subject is in English, the interpretation should first be in English, also because they're dealing with theories in English and it's included in the board exam. Even the English subject is included in the board exam.]

Salient in Ms Helena's and Mr Gregorio's response is the conception of English as the language of technical knowledge. It is the language in which accounting and business theories are presented in instructional materials, such as reference books, which sometimes include supplementary resources such as lesson notes in PowerPoint files that teachers can use as visual aids in their lectures. It is the language in which the commonly used disciplinary lexicon (e.g. 'assets', 'liabilities') is coded, thus supporting the notion that English is the language of accounting, and consequently, the medium that is best suited to teach the discipline.

The value of English is further reified as the language of tests in university (for all content courses) and post-university, the most important of which is the Certified Public Accountant (CPA) licensure exam, the mandatory qualification for professional practice. Besides having all items framed in English, a mini-language test has been included in the CPA qualifying exam since 2016 as part of the revisions issued by the Professional Regulatory Board of Accountancy (BoA). Among the updates detailed in the BoA Resolution No. 275, Series 2015, 'effective communication to stakeholders' was added to the list of topics in the Taxation test. This topic is covered by four items in English grammar and usage. Albeit minimal, the explicit testing of language in the licensure exam raises the already high status ascribed to English. Collectively, the prevalence of English in instructional materials and tests perpetuates the power and prestige of the language and those who can display competence in it (Shohamy, 2006).

Shohamy (2006) explains that de facto practices like these are even more potent than formal language policy because their effect is not easily perceived. Social actors are unaware that 'the very fact of using one language and not another… sends a direct message as to the de facto priority of one language over another. This is being accepted as a given with no resistance and no negotiations' (Shohamy, 2006: 55). Another hidden effect of these normalized practices is seen in how teachers are motivated to focus on teaching the 'test language' as they tend to interpret students' performance in tests as a reflection of their teaching effectiveness. In fact, accounting schools consider the CPA board exam results as an important measure of the education quality they provide and proudly publicize passing percentages and topnotchers that they produce (Tolentino-Baysa, 2015).

One marked way that this test language is taught to students in content classes is by designating English as the preferred language for students' formal performance of specialized knowledge. Written outputs submitted by students and oral presentations they do in class are delivered in English. This was demonstrated in Ms Diwata's class where she

Table 4.1 Communicative function of teacher utterances in Filipino

Communicative function	Teacher utterances in Filipino
1. To engage students to recite or participate in discussion	*Anong sagot dito?* [What's the answer here?] *Anong ibig sabihin nun,* class? [What does that mean, class?]
2. To check students' understanding	Okay *ba?* [Is it okay?] *Malinaw ha?* [Clear, yes?]
3. To give evaluative comments about the lesson	*Wag muna nating ipasok baka magulo ang inyong pag-iisip.* [Let's not include it for now because it might confuse you.] *Simple lang!* [It's simple!]
4. To give feedback on student behavior	*Anong nginingiti-ngiti mo diyan?* [What are you smiling about?] *Kinalimutan na!* [Forgotten already!]
5. To reformulate a question originally framed in English	*Magkano* adjustment *mo dito*? [How much do you adjust here?] *Sino yung huling nag-log in sa* cloud? [Who was the last one to log into the cloud?]
6. To explain, illustrate or simplify a concept	*Bayad muna bago upa hindi upa muna bago bayad.* [Pay first before renting, not rent first before paying.] *Ang drama niyo naman,* sir. *Bilin niyo na lang.* [You are too dramatic, sir. Just buy it.]

promptly reminded the reporting student to explain his answer in English. The student, who started his presentation in Filipino, then immediately shifted to English.

While English is viewed as the 'ideal' and 'proper' medium for teacher and student presentation of specialized knowledge, the L1 of social actors (here, Filipino) also plays a role in knowledge communication. Table 4.1 shows expressions made by content teachers in Filipino and their communicative functions.

These Filipino expressions exemplify the auxiliary functions of L1 in instruction. To explain the supportive role of Filipino in content delivery, Mr Fernando (accounting teacher) uses a performance metaphor.

Excerpt 4.10

Mr Fernando: (...) *support lang. Hindi siya dapat* main. *Hindi siya yung* superstar *pero ma-aassure lang sila na naiintidihan nila.* [(...) it's just support. It should not be the main one. It's not the superstar but it is to assure that the students understand.]

The discourse compares Filipino to a sidekick, the constant yet subordinate companion of the superstar – the part played by English. As described, Filipino is a back-up medium used to fill gaps in lesson delivery and comprehension that cannot be successfully accomplished by social actors in the main language, English. This is particularly clear in the recasting of questions in Filipino when students were unresponsive to the interrogatives in English and in shifting to Filipino when discussing concepts that need to be simplified or emphasized. Such strategic use of Filipino addresses the problem of students' hesitance to ask and answer questions, which Airey (2009) also observed in Swedish universities where physics teachers lectured in English. He mentioned students' lack of confidence in their comprehension of the question, and fear of their limited fluency in English being exposed as reasons for their apprehension to participate in class. This knowledge and linguistic insecurity is managed by teachers in my study by shifting to the students' and their own L1 (Filipino).

The other noted functions of Filipino in teacher talk, while not directly involving content, are pedagogically relevant as they relate to teaching methods and affect learning. Posing questions to elicit student response, checking whether they understand the lesson, and commenting on the lesson and student behavior are ways that teachers monitor how students receive the knowledge presented to them.

On the part of students, they also used Filipino in content-related conversations. Students were commonly heard using mostly this L1 during small group discussions. For instance, during a group seatwork activity in Mr Carlos' class, the students conversed with each other mainly in Filipino. With their textbook, worksheet, calculator and pen, students sat on their armchairs arranged into small circles and discussed the assigned case studies, saying things such as, '*Hindi ko rin ma-so-solve ito* [I can't solve this either]' and '*Isusulat ko lang yung admin expense* [I'll just write the admin expense]'. This demonstrates the use of Filipino as the medium in processing the knowledge targeted in the course. According to first-year accounting student Nico, switching to the mother tongue is helpful because discussions in monolingual English can be 'difficult for the brain'.

The described scenarios in this section suggest that English and Filipino are applied meaningfully by teachers and students to communicate knowledge. They generally employed English as medium to present knowledge (in instructional materials, lectures) and assess knowledge (in student oral reports, written tests), and added Filipino to help process knowledge (e.g. monitoring student understanding during lectures, group seatwork discussions). This observation is consistent with Tamtomo (2018) who noted that Indonesian vocational teachers allowed multilingualism in the learning process but required students' final products and performance of learning to be monolingual. Schooled in these language practices, accounting students also recognize English as the more formal medium, which is generally appropriate when addressing their teachers. But unlike the monoglot ideology dominantly held by Chinese and Hong Kong university students in Gu's (2014) study, these Filipino accounting students do not see translanguaging in the classroom as inconsistent with the communication goals of the program.

The observed use of linguistic codes shows that language choice in the accounting classroom is intentional and reflects two key beliefs – that English is the language of globalized accounting and that learning is easier and more effective in the students' L1. Essentially, English is treated as the primary transactional language for exchanging field knowledge (O'Keeffe *et al.*, 2007). However, between teacher presentation of information and student display of acquired knowledge, Filipino takes the important role of broker language, negotiating communication gaps in the teaching and learning process. Parallel to these knowledge-focused activities, classroom interactions also evince interpersonally motivated communication, which I now turn to.

4.4 Communicating Relationships

The notion of relational language, introduced by O'Keeffe *et al.* (2007: 159), refers to 'language which serves to create and maintain good relations between the speaker and hearer'. While this kind of talk has a distinct communicative aim, it is found to co-occur with transactional talk. In the accounting classroom particularly, students and teachers are observed to do interpersonal work through language while engaged in pedagogical exchange.

In the same group seatwork activity in Mr Carlos' class, where students collaborated to solve an assigned accounting problem (described earlier in Section 4.3), I heard them occasionally shifting their discussion from task on hand to some other unrelated subject. For instance, a student told her groupmate, '*Kaklase yan ng kapatid ko eh* [That's my sibling's classmate]!' This utterance demonstrates casual talk.

Using a shared L1 to do social talk is particularly common practice in what Goffman (1990: 114) calls 'back region' or 'back stage' – those unmonitored, private moments where students are able to discuss unofficial or personal matters in the classroom. Accounting students Maria and Jaya confirmed that they use Filipino when talking to their friends in class about informal topics, demonstrating that L1 is the instinctive medium of friendly talk among peers. This inclination informs the belief of Ms Edna, a Filipino language teacher, that students can best develop their interpersonal communication skills if they use their 'own language', that is, the language in which they are most comfortable, in this case Filipino.

Students, however, are not the only ones who use Filipino for relational communication. Teachers also use Filipino to establish rapport with their students. The desire to present themselves as both knowledgeable and approachable is particularly salient during the first meeting of the term, where course introduction and impression management are the main items in the teacher's agenda. This attempt to simultaneously achieve transactional and relational goals is observed in the accounting class of Mr Gregorio.

In the first meeting of the term, Mr Gregorio briefly introduced the course. After explaining the unit objectives, he randomly called two students to explain why they took up accounting. Since he was not yet familiar with the students' names, he referred to them as '*Ate*', the Filipino vocative for 'older sister', which is commonly used outside the family domain to express politeness and engender familiarity with any woman regardless of age. The first student stood up and began explaining that it has been her childhood dream to become a lawyer and that she is taking up accounting as a pre-law course. When the student hesitated to proceed with her answer, Mr Gregorio encouraged her, '*Sige lang, walang wrong answer.* [Go ahead. There's no wrong answer.]' The student then finished her response in Filipino. Calling on another student, Mr Gregorio reframed his original question, '*Anong nakikita mo sa* career path *mo*? [What do you envision in your career path?]' The second student promptly responded in Filipino.

This brief exchange, which focuses on students' motivation for their degree choice, is more relational than transactional. By allowing students to talk about their own reasons for taking up accounting, the teacher creates space for personal narratives to be expressed and cultivate feelings of solidarity in class – among students who potentially share similar motivations and with the teacher who levels with them. The use of '*Ate*' to address the students, which is more commonly done among peers, may be seen as the teacher's effort to orient himself with students in a more social or relational way. He continues to build rapport by using this L1 to support students in their participation. By way of modeling, he frames an encouragement and reformulates the question in the language with which the students are presumably more comfortable. This linguistic choice, which the students adopt, is motivated by a desire for students to perceive his accounting class as a safe space, where they are free to express themselves. Mr Gregorio confirms that he shifted to Filipino to make the students feel relaxed as it is the first meeting. He even disclosed that if I had not been around, he might have told more jokes in Filipino. Besides the observer's paradox, this comment makes explicit the value of Filipino as language of humor and connection.

The priority of rapport building, however, is not limited to the beginning of the term. In a midterm meeting with one of his accounting classes, Mr Carlo markedly shifted to Filipino to make casual comments, such as noticing a student's new haircut and lipstick and adjusting the room temperature. Such comments create an informal mood suggesting the teacher's concern for students beyond their engagement in subject matter learning. It gives the notion that the teacher sees his students as individual persons – he notices changes in their look and is concerned about their physical comfort in class. When asked about the reason for his use of Filipino and occasionally some other Philippine languages, Mr Carlo explained that he uses local languages that are part of his students' linguistic repertoire, 'Ilocano terms because we have Ilocano students... Bisaya because we also have Bisaya students. Ilonggo because you also have Ilonggo students. And they like that'. This response makes explicit the teacher's deference to what students like, potentially to serve the higher pedagogical purpose of motivating their learning. Kriselda and Lorenzo find Mr Carlo's multilingual teaching style 'very effective' as it piques their interest and aids their understanding. L1 is thus linked with the genuineness of the teacher's desire to help students learn.

Using Filipino to encourage learning was also demonstrated by Mr Fernando, who consciously maintained a positive learning atmosphere in his advanced accounting class. He managed the affective filter of his students by saying '*Relax lang. Inom muna ng tubig.* [Just relax. Drink water first.]' as he advanced to the next topic. He also used positive metaphors like '*Para bang nayayakap mo yung* dollars. [It's as if you can embrace the dollars.]' in explaining technical concepts. This may be viewed as the use of L1 to support content, as well as an effort to create positive feelings in class, which is a key feature of interpersonal communication.

So far, the class interactions described featured teachers' initiatives to establish and maintain rapport with students. Albeit minimally observed, students also use Filipino to establish rapport with their teacher. Interestingly, this was demonstrated in Ms Aurora's English class, where EOP is explicitly enforced. This language rule, however, appears to be relaxed during small group discussions where students act in a carefree manner. Some students sat on the table and used their mobile phones while brainstorming. One group was especially lively, joking around and laughing. When Ms Aurora approached this group, the students consulted her mostly in English. Then, a student said, '*Ang ganda nun*, Miss, *noh*? [Isn't it beautiful, Miss?]' This comment, framed in Filipino, aims to solicit positive feedback from Ms Aurora, who however did not verbally acknowledge the question and simply walked over to the next group. In this case, it is the student who shifted to Filipino seemingly to engage the teacher in small talk, a feature of relational language (O'Keeffe *et al.*, 2007). The silence appears to be a rejection of the attempt to casually relate to the teacher, perhaps to maintain the traditional formality in teacher–student relation. Although seemingly unsuccessful, this example provides further evidence of Filipino as the primary language of rapport and relationship in class interaction.

Albeit less prominent, relational talk in English is also noted in two instances. One example is Mr Fernando, who occasionally complimented his students using stock expressions in English, such as 'I'm proud of you' and 'Exactly, I'm happy for you'. In both instances, the students responded with laughter. Another example is the student in Ms Diwata's accounting class, who was told to explain his computation in English (reported in Section 4.3). Obligingly, the student shifted to English and restarted his report by addressing his classmates with the casual vocative 'Guys' – which elicited laughter. Before he could continue, Ms Diwata told him to move to the side so that the class could see what he had written on the board. He responded, 'Yes, Ma'am'. Then, to his classmates, he said, 'Are you seeing?' Again, everyone laughed.

These two cases feature relational talk in English addressed publicly, that is, to the whole class as opposed to an individual person or a small group. In both instances, the group laughter suggests shared ideologies about the language used. Laughter in these scenarios may be interpreted as an index of amusement at the teacher's atypical use of English for complimenting and soliciting feedback, which are more routinely performed in Filipino (see Section 4.3). In the case of Ms Diwata's student, the laughter his final utterance invoked may be directed toward the ungrammaticality of the sentence, 'Are you seeing?' (instead of 'Can you see?'). Interpreted this way, the token may be viewed as an informal way of noticing or correcting the error. On the other hand, it may be a face-saving mechanism employed by his peers to soften the impact of the potentially shaming public correction by the teacher. Another possibility is that the student and his classmates are engaged in what Jørgensen (2008: 172) describes as 'a mutual activity of poking fun at the world'.

Here, the speaker may be intentionally making fun of English by shifting to the prescribed language in a joking manner; his peers participate in the fun by acknowledging the humor. This is similar to how call center agents in Salonga's (2010) study reported mocking English by deliberately 'bastardizing' it in the unmonitored back stage.

Interactional evidence presented in this section shows that relational language overlaps with transactional talk in the classroom. Teachers and students are variably invested in establishing and maintaining positive social relations with each other while collaborating to transfer and acquire knowledge. Social goals in class interaction are commonly achieved through the use of L1 (Filipino), as noted also by Tamtomo (2018: 446), who found that L1 (in her study, Javanese) 'closes the social distance between teacher and student'. In my study, Filipino – the predominant L1 – is indexed as the language of ease and comfort, which is used to create or express a desire for closeness. As accounting student Olivia describes, 'When the professors use Tagalog, it has a more personal touch when they try to explain things to help the student better understand the lesson'. Hence, teachers' use of Filipino tends to be viewed as relationally oriented even though it may be transactionally motivated.

Whereas Filipino is seen as the language of friendship in class, English is used to introduce fun or the element of play in knowledge presentation. Laughing at compliments in English indexes a kind of shared attempt by students as well as teachers to designate it as a supplementary medium of relationships in addition to being the primary medium of transaction. One of the key themes of transactional exchange in the classroom, which focuses on teachers' valuing of students' language preparation for accounting work, was briefly discussed in Section 4.2. The next section offers a closer look at this highlighted communication practice and ideology.

4.5 Communicating Signs of Work Competence

The priority of neoliberal accounting education is to equip students with knowledge needed in their target profession, which they can leverage in the highly competitive new economy corporate sector. This involves communicating information about what it means to be an accountant in this present time, what the workplace is like, what tasks they are likely to engage in, and what abilities and qualities are valued in the corporate sector. Advice on signs of competence in accounting practice is variably shaped by teachers' knowledge of the field.

Table 4.2 provides an overview of the teacher participants based on the extent of their engagement in the accounting or business fields of practice. Here, practitioner teachers are distinguished from academic teachers. The first type has two subtypes: current (those who are actively employed in accounting and business work at the time of data collection)

Table 4.2 Types of teachers

Practitioner teachers		Academic teachers
Current practitioners	**Former practitioners**	
Mr Basilio (Accounting)	Mr Carlo (Accounting)	Ms Aurora, PhD (English)
	Ms Diwata, PhD (Accounting)	Ms Edna (Filipino)
	Mr Fernando (Accounting)	
	Mr Gregorio (Accounting)	
	Ms Helena (Business)	

and former practitioners (those who were previously engaged in the disciplinal field).

The table indicates three types of teachers in accounting schools. Current practitioner teachers are part-time academics holding full-time positions in accounting practice. They rarely have PhD qualifications but hold key career positions as senior directors or partners. As part-time faculty, they are classified as lecturers (guest, assistant, senior, professional or senior professional lecturer). The second type of teachers are former practitioners, who have previous practitioner experience but are currently full-time academics holding master's or doctoral degrees in their fields of specialization. Finally, academic teachers have purely academic experience (teaching) and qualifications (MA or PhD degrees). As full-time faculty, both former practitioner and academic teachers are ranked as professors (assistant, associate or full professor). I discuss in turn how teachers belonging to each category variably prepare future accountants to communicate in the workplace.

4.5.1 Current practitioner teacher

Presently involved in the workplace that the students are targeting to join, the current practitioner teacher capitalized on his firsthand knowledge of the field as a basis for decisions about what and how to teach students to communicate.

Excerpt 4.11

Mr Basilio: (...) based on my experience as a teacher here, well I think you'll be able to effectively impart to the students the knowledge if you have experience. (...) I'm also telling the faculty sometimes that, well, you have to impart practical things well to your students so that they'll be able to appreciate what you're actually teaching.

(...)

Mr Basilio: (...) sometimes I'm not actually impressed by some of the faculty who have a master's degree or PhD. (...) Well for me I actually value more experience because I think it is from experience that you actually gain a lot.

In this excerpt, Mr Basilio refers to two kinds of experience: teaching ('my experience as a teacher') and accounting practice. He emphasizes the latter as more valuable in transferring knowledge that is practical for students' preparation for work and that is more impressive than knowledge represented by higher academic degrees. He constructs his professional background as partner in a prestigious Philippine-based auditing firm with strong international linkages as a symbolic capital to assert his status among academically credentialed teachers.

This practice of using one's practitioner experience as a discursive means of building credibility mirrors the stance of 'self-appointed Putnamian experts' – based on Putnam's 1975 study of language and notions of 'real' – who position themselves as authorities in discerning whether a particular subject is authentic or fake (Reyes, 2017: 102). In this case, Mr Basilio contends that traditional academic qualifications (MA, PhD) sans practitioner experience represent limited expertise in discerning what happens in the 'real world', which is constructed as a composite of the workplace and other social domains outside school. He maintains this discourse of distinction between sites (academia vs practice) and expertise (academic vs practitioner teachers) by deploying the 'experience' trope to make a case for his own communication training practices in class.

Excerpt 4.12

Mr Basilio: (…) during the faculty meetings, sometimes I also share my experiences in the office so sometimes I tell them that the students don't know how to write business letters. (…) Because sometimes, well of course in the office you have to write business letters, right? Sometimes just simple format of the business letter they [the students] don't know.

(…)

Mr Basilio: (…) normally I tell them that when they write a written report, it should be in business English. So it should not be technical English. So the English should be easily understood by the reader. (…) it should be in active voice, not in passive voice.

(…)

Mr Basilio: I require my students to speak in English because I know that in the workplace English is actually needed. (…) well particularly in [Company], well even our staff when they do presentation, they [partners] are actually requiring them to speak in English. (…) they [staff] have to speak in English while lecturing because if there's a partner that's actually attending the session and then they're actually speaking not in English, well sometimes the partner will actually tell them that they have to speak in English.

Citing authentic communication practices in the firm where he is partner, Mr Basilio prescribes that accounting students be taught how to format business letters, use business English, and speak in English. His insistence on monolingual English is supported by imagined scenarios of workplace interactions with people holding higher career status relative to accounting students' projected future selves.

Holding the top position in a commonly desired job destination of newly graduated accountants, Mr Basilio uses the work experience discourse as a strategy to assert his authority on how to communicate effectively not only in the students' target domain (workplace) but also in the current site (school). This strategy operates by highlighting the prestige of the current practitioner's occupation-informed knowledge, which suggests an authority differential between practitioner and nonpractitioner teachers. In the process, the experience-based advice is framed as value-adding knowledge that represents the gap or what is missing in purely 'textbook-based' instruction.

4.5.2 Former practitioner teachers

Representing occupation knowledge through their previous involvement in accounting work, former practitioner teachers also deployed the work experience trope to support the communication advice they dispensed to students.

Excerpt 4.13

Mr Carlo: (...) if I see a gentleman, a guy who is wearing white socks with a slacks and the formal *balat* [leather] shoes on, I would say of course you should not wear that unless you are Michael Jackson. (...) When you go to the workplace, packaging is also communication. The way you architect your image, the way you manage your image is also communication.

(...)

Mr Carlo: (...) a huge influence about that for me perhaps because my first employer was [Company]. So packaging is very, very important. The way you project yourself to your client.

In this excerpt, Mr Carlo focuses on the physical aspects of self-presentation as part of acceptable ways of communicating in the workplace, driving his point that 'packaging is also communication'. He mentions his experience with his first employer, another big accounting firm in the Philippines with international linkages, to justify his attention to how students dress for work-like class activities (e.g. group presentations as simulation of client presentation). As the official trainer of students participating in inter-school competitions (where students make business case presentations), he ensures that his students know the do's and don'ts of modern corporate fashion.

Another former practitioner, Mr Fernando, deploys his expertise in corporate communication through role-play. After explaining an accounting concept, he dramatized an imagined dialogue between an accountant and a client to show how students should explain numbers in a way that is meaningful and helpful to nonaccountants. This 'reflexive performance' (Reyes, 2017: 122) features a physical enactment or, more precisely, a linguistic demonstration of communicative competence in the corporate setting focusing on vocabulary for accountant–client interactions.

Both Mr Carlo and Mr Fernando provided advice on surface features of communication, such as dress code and word choice, which are 'typical' – that is, easy to replicate – markers of corporate membership (Reyes, 2017). While also built on the authority of work experience, the occupation-specific knowledge exchanged by these former practitioners appears limited compared with those offered by the current practitioner. This suggests the valuing of up-to-date knowledge, that is, the more current the practitioner experience, the more authentic and extensive the advice and the more credible the teacher's authority. The conditions of authority (Piller, 2019) and teaching strategies, however, are different in general education classes, where teachers are nonpractitioners.

4.5.3 Academic teachers

Generally, academic teachers' authority is based on their academic qualification in their area of specialization, such that a PhD indexes having the highest authority on the subject or unit. However, in the case of accounting schools, academic teachers appeared to follow the pattern of leveraging the value of professional knowledge. This is exemplified in an assessment task that Ms Edna designed for her Filipino language class.

Excerpt 4.14

Ms Edna: (...) *parang* documentary *yung* final output (...) *Mag-iinterview sila ng* expert *para ma*-realize *nila na paano mo magagamit yung* Filipino. And then *ang gusto ko talaga sa kanila* eventually *makapunta sila sa mga* grassroots, *halimbawa yung mga tindera. Kasi kelangan din nila ng* accounting *dun, di ba?* [(...) their final output will be like a documentary (...) They will interview an expert to realize how they use Filipino in the job. And then, I envision that they will eventually go to the grassroots, for example small vendors because they also need accounting. Don't they?]

The course capstone project described by Ms Edna requires students to interact with actual entrepreneurs – 'real experts' – to inquire into the use of Filipino language in their work. Her references to 'grassroots' and 'small vendors' reflect ideologies about the relation of language and social class, specifically where Filipino is linked to small-scale, local enterprises whereas English – as attested by the current practitioner – is associated with large global businesses.

Such invitation to interact with experts and to imagine their professional selves is also typified in a group activity in Ms Aurora's English oral communication class, where she required students to stage a talk show where they take on the role of experts in their respective fields. Since students in this class are enrolled in different business courses (e.g. legal, management, marketing and accounting), a variety of jobs were represented in the panel. In this task, Jaya, an accounting student, portrayed the role of a CPA who is vice president of finance for a manufacturing corporation. Enacting this part entailed researching and role-playing the expertise of a CPA using a memorized script.

Both documentary and talk show tasks are assessments in language classes, where the teachers are not 'disciplinary insiders' (Airey, 2011: 1), nonexperts in the accounting field. Having limited knowledge of occupation-specific communicative practices, these academic teachers introduced the 'work experience' dimension in their unit by designing assessments that involve students interacting with practitioners and reporting knowledge about professional communication. Students then perform their knowledge about workplace communication practices in scripted formats such as documentary and talk show. Then, capitalizing on their certified knowledge as language experts, teachers provide input and feedback based on general principles of communicative competence, including speaking audibly, speaking within the given time, and using open gestures to project confidence.

This practice shows that academic teachers, despite having higher academic qualifications, are seemingly discredited by their lack of firsthand knowledge on workplace communication practices. The language teachers' strategic inclusion of this component in assessments reflects an attempt to meet students' expectations of 'real-world' communication training and to negotiate their teacher authority as experts in specific languages and in general communication.

Overall, interactional and interview data indicate that differentially credentialed teachers have distinctive ways of advising students on what counts as communicative competence in the accounting field. More importantly, they provide evidence that teachers view their academic and professional identities (credentialed by degrees and work experience) as conditions of authority (Piller, 2019).

The analysis demonstrates that while differentially positioned to deploy advice on workplace communication competence markers, practitioner and academic teachers similarly target developing in students what Airey (2011: 3) calls 'disciplinary literacy [which] refers to the ability to appropriately participate in the communicative practices of [the] discipline'. Teachers use what resources are available to them (professional capital for practitioner teachers, and academic capital for academic teachers) to propose a notion of students' future professional selves tied to their role as communicators.

The imagined communication practices of accountants, including the languages, skills and tasks involved in the job, are differentially constructed based on teachers' knowledge of the field. Having firsthand and up-to-date knowledge of the profession, the current practitioner teacher positions himself as being most credible to 'disambiguat[e] disciplinary communicative practices' (Airey, 2011: 1). As such, his (as well as other practitioner teachers') communication training strategies (e.g. EOP, business English) tend to be viewed as value-adding. They are seen as an alignment of academic and corporate practices, which are typically constructed as worlds apart as suggested by 'real world' and 'work experience' discourses.

Practitioner teachers' professional capital leverages their authority and credibility, which may appear self-appointed (because of explicit and repeated deployment of the 'work experience' trope) but is essentially institutionally conferred (Piller, 2019). The institutional conferral of academic authority to practitioner teachers is partly indicated by the percentage of current practitioner teachers employed in one of the participating schools. The faculty profile published in the university website shows that nearly 80% of accounting teachers are active practitioners. The same profile also shows that less than 15% of accounting teachers are PhD holders. These numbers suggest that having accounting work experience exempts faculty members from academic qualifications traditionally required for university teaching positions. While they are given less prestigious academic ranks as lecturers (not professors), their professional credentials render their knowledge more superior on matters relating to the accounting field, including what counts as 'effective' communication.

Academic education literature acknowledges the institutional habitus favoring practical experience over academic preparation of faculty members (e.g. Johnson, 2014; Mounce *et al.*, 2004). This habitus predisposes practitioner teachers to be viewed favorably as 'more helpful and influential than those with purely academic credentials' in providing students a 'smooth entry point into the profession' (Johnson, 2014: 111, 109).

In sum, what signs of corporate competence are articulated and how they are articulated by teachers are tied to practitioner and academic teachers' representation of their authority as knowledge source. In this shared position, teachers differentially leverage their professional and academic qualifications to prepare students to communicate as accountants.

4.6 Summary

Overall, this analysis reveals that communication practices in accounting classrooms are shaped mainly by the pedagogical aim to prepare students to become competent accountants capable of performing specialized knowledge numerically and communicatively. Referring to the latter, I borrow Airey's (2011) concept of 'disciplinary literacy' and use it in this context as the ability to competently participate in communicative practices in the accounting profession. In developing students' disciplinary literacy, multiple language ideologies and practices are enacted in classroom interactions. Prominent are communication practices that are tied to ideological tensions related to present academic needs and future professional aspirations, differential valuing of English and Filipino as languages of technical knowledge and rapport, and teachers' strategic leveraging of their general and occupation-specific knowledge of professional communication.

Classroom language use and management are shaped by the nature of the subject and two pedagogical aims that are differentially prioritized by teachers – ensuring students' comprehension of content and developing their proficiency in the language of their target profession. These two goals are linked to different languages and reflect ideologies about English as the language of future professional communication and bilingualism in English and Filipino as beneficial in addressing present teaching and learning needs. At the junction of this ideological tension, teachers contend between prescribing monolingual English as practice for professional communication, which however may complicate students' learning of present subject matter; or allowing bilingual practices to effectively transfer academic content while potentially delaying improvement of students' fluency in the main language of their future job. In negotiating the simultaneous production of students' disciplinary literacy in the academic context here and now and for the future workplace, languages are ideologically hierarchized.

English and Filipino are differentially positioned as languages of knowledge and relationships. Their status relative to each other varies depending on the transactional or interpersonal orientation of the communication event. Where the focus is communicating knowledge, English takes center stage as the veritable 'superstar', the front stage language for the performance of technical competence. Meanwhile, Filipino is compared to a sidekick, the constant yet subordinate companion that performs various auxiliary functions to aid instruction. On the other hand, where the focus is communicating the social intentions of establishing rapport and maintaining positive relations, the status of the languages is reversed. Filipino takes precedence as the main language of friendship among social actors who share it as their L1 while English takes the supportive role as alternative medium for rapport through complimenting and joking. Since transactional talk and relational talk in classroom discourse are often intertwined, shifts in the status of English and Filipino occur instantaneously. Yet English continues to be designated the more prestigious status socially as the language of accounting, which has the effect of erasing credit to the role of Filipino.

The resounding discourse of English as the language of globalized accounting is an example of professional communication knowledge that is deployed by differentially credentialed teachers. Practitioner teachers use 'real world' and 'work experience' discourse to promote this language ideology. Meanwhile, academic (especially language) teachers design assessments for students to enact or negotiate the hegemonic view of English as the language of professional success in the accounting field.

The reported communication practices of teachers and accounting students indicate an intentionality that is tied to their shared desire to sufficiently prepare students to participate in the accounting field. An important contribution of this analysis is the foregrounding of language hierarchization in the classroom, which is tied to social actors' ideologically driven bilingual practices and to teachers' experience-based claims of how language works in the target profession. This finding suggests that teachers' 'real-world' experience of accounting work is an important knowledge capital in higher education that challenges traditional views of language teachers as authority in communication training.

The second part of this book moves the discussion to the post-university trajectory of accounting students: the accounting workplace and what ways and views of communication are present in this professional domain.

Part 2

Communication in Accounting Work

5 'Effective Communication' as Criterion for Employment

5.1 Introduction

This chapter begins to investigate spoken and written communication practices and ideologies in globalized accounting work. Following the pattern of inquiry adopted in school sites (discussed in Chapters 3 and 4), I explore the professional context by first examining the view of employers, social actors at the top of the field hierarchy, reflected in 135 recruitment ads (36 for onshore and 99 for offshore accountant positions). Sourced from a career website for online jobs and company websites of top accounting firms and private companies in the Philippines, these ads comprise the 37,095-word corpus examined in a two-part analysis. First, I identify significant language patterns and salient themes around the key term 'communication' as a way to understand what communicative resources are prioritized by gatekeepers in their hiring intention. Then, probing the ideologies of communication in globalized accounting work, I examine how different notions of communication in the job ads are mobilized in corporate hiring practices as experienced by employers and accountants.

5.2 The Construction of 'Communication' in Online Job Ads

Job advertisements, a text produced by organizations primarily to recruit new members, constitute an important resource to understand what qualities are valued in globalized accounting work. At the same time, job adverts serve as a public relations document, a metaphorical window offering a fashioned view of the organization (Rafaeli & Oliver, 1998). As both recruitment and marketing device, these work notices represent a discourse where ideologies about the desired workers and workplace identity are normalized (Fairclough, 2010). My interest is how the idea of communication as a condition for organizational membership is encoded in this ritualized text, potentially offering a view into ideologies about what is considered 'effective communication' in accounting work.

5.2.1 Structural positioning of 'communication'

Structure provides a logical starting point for this textual analysis. Studies so far have mostly focused on classified print ads marked by five elements: (1) target (title of the job vacancy), (2) recruiter (information about the employer and the duties involved in the advertised role), (3) requirements (minimum qualifications for the job), (4) reward (promised salary and benefits) and (5) contact (gatekeeper's name and telephone number) (Bruthiaux, 1996; Rafaeli & Oliver, 1998). I adopt these elements in my analysis of online job ads while mindful that the affordances of online media enable greater structural flexibility (Sodhi & Son, 2010).

Table 5.1 shows the elements I identified in the structure of the corpus. As shown, the elements consistently present in job posts for globalized accounting work are the human resource needs (variably labeled 'job overview', 'job description' or 'job summary') and the job requirements (or 'skills required'). Meanwhile, the other elements are variably represented in offshore and onshore job ads. A unique element seen in these ads, what I labeled 'pre-test', is an assessment designed to prescreen candidates and validate their ability to perform some required skills. This takes various forms, such as a 'challenge', which consists of a series of tasks for the applicant to accomplish (see Excerpt 5.10), or a list of questions to be answered, or mandatory test outcomes (e.g. 'English test result of C1 or C2'). These pre-tests are designed to ensure that the applicant has carefully considered the job posting and, as explained by one of the job ads, 'to filter everyone out and find out if you are THE ONE we are looking for' [emphasis in the original]. As this pre-test is seen in only one onshore job ad, it may be considered as a more distinctive feature of offshore online job ads.

This feature and variations in the salience of other elements may be attributed to factors such as the organization's reputation and the online modality of the recruitment process. What appears more definitive is the salience of 'human resource needs' and 'job requirements' not only as mandatory elements across the corpus but also as the

Table 5.1 Elements in online job ads for accountants

Elements	Offshore job ads (*n* = 99)	Onshore job ads (*n* = 36)
Company identity	76 (77%)	36 (100%)
Human resource needs	**99 (100%)**	**36 (100%)**
Job requirements	**99 (100%)**	**36 (100%)**
Reward	99 (100%)	10 (28%)
Contact details	12 (12%)	6 (17%)
Pre-test	20 (20%)	1 (3%)

Table 5.2 Frequency of skills terms in online job ads

Skills	Number of tokens in offshore job ads	Number of tokens in onshore job ads	Total
accounting	254	66	320
management	202	66	268
finance	114	26	140
bookkeeping	126	1	127
tax	105	17	122
QuickBooks	80	–	80
English	72	6	78
Xero	73	3	76
payroll	71	2	73
admin	58	1	59
writing	43	–	43
speaking	41	–	41
communication	24	13	37

components of the text where 'communication' is positioned. This pattern veritably situates communication at the center of the commodifying process where candidates self-evaluate against the specified requirements and view themselves as more or less embodying the desired 'bundle of skills' (Urciuoli, 2008).

To concretize the salience of 'communication' and other skills required for accountant positions, the word list of the corpus was checked, revealing the frequencies shown in Table 5.2.

The table shows that technical skills related to field knowledge ('accounting', 'management', 'finance', 'bookkeeping', 'tax', 'payroll') as well as accounting software ('QuickBooks', 'Xero') are mentioned much more frequently than 'communication' and other related skills ('writing', 'speaking'). The only communication-related term that is comparably as recurrent as some technical knowledge-based skills is 'English'. While generally less recurrent, reference to this language and other communication terms ('writing', 'speaking', 'communication') suggests an interest in the linguistic capital that accountants bring into the workplace, echoing curricular rhetoric. To explore the semantic value of communication in this context, I examine its enregisterments or the referring expressions used in the text that shape how the notion is interpreted (Urciuoli, 2008, 2010). Specifically, I explore patterns of use that emerge from the use of three corpus analytical techniques – collocates, word clusters and keywords in context (KWIC). This approach parallels the textual analysis carried out on the accountancy program documents in Chapter 3.

5.2.2 Patterned use of 'communication'

Collocates is the first tool used to examine the corpus. Frequently co-occurring words can point to important social practices in the field where the examined corpus is created and circulated. Probing this language pattern can provide evidence of the way that a group of people has been socialized to communicate (Handford, 2015). Hence, collocations are potentially significant indicators of ideologies held by employers of globalized accountants.

The strongest collocates of 'communication' were identified by setting the minimum frequency to 5, which is the prescribed level for determining significant collocates (see also Section 3.3). The lexical items shown in Table 5.3 are the top-ranking items resulting from this quantitative test.

The concordance lines of these collocates evince conventionalized phrasing that melds writing and speaking together (Collocates 1, 3 and 4) and links evaluative descriptors to these forms of communication (Collocates 5, 6, 7, 9 and 10). 'Presentation' (Collocate 2) or the reporting of work outputs stands out as a specific work task where these 'skills' (Collocate 8) may be performed. In terms of language, 'English' (Collocate 11) is the only identified medium for corporate communication.

After identifying individual words that frequently co-occur, I examined next clusters or n-grams, which are contiguous sequences of words that are highly frequent and dispersed in the corpus. Setting the minimum frequency to 5 and the minimum range (number of files where the clusters appear) to 10 revealed five significantly recurrent word clusters, shown in Table 5.4.

The combination of words resulting from this test indicates that the advertised positions entail communicating disciplinal information in

Table 5.3 Top lexical collocates of 'communication'

Rank	Statistical strength of collocation	Collocate
1	9.70017	verbal
2	9.24449	presentation
3	9.07457	oral
4	8.92256	written
5	8.92256	advanced
6	8.63716	excellent
7	8.54405	effective
8	7.15960	skills
9	6.48960	strong
10	6.46313	good
11	5.95909	English

Table 5.4 N-grams related to communication

N-Gram	Tokens in offshore job ads	Tokens in onshore job ads	Total
writing finance management accounting	31	1	32
English speaking writing finance	14	11	25
speaking writing finance management	25	–	25
skills required English speaking	21	–	21
required English speaking writing	15	–	15
	106	12	118

Table 5.5 Communication keywords in offshore and onshore job ads

Keywords	Offshore job ads	Onshore job ads
Speaking and writing	writing, speaking	
Technology	email, online, internet, virtual	
Language	English	
Relationships		team/s, relationships, teamwork

English. This finding is consistent with the analysis of collocates, which bears out three themes: (1) written communication, (2) spoken communication and (3) communicating in English. Using the concordance tool to investigate the context of these clusters reveals that 90% of these communication-related lexical bundles are found in ads for offshore accountant positions.

To investigate other unique enregisterments of 'communication' in onshore and offshore job ads, I compared the two subcorpora using KWIC. The KWIC test results (shown in Table 5.5) highlights words related to 'communication' that are unusually frequent in each subcorpus. Items relating to the same notion of communication are grouped together.

The KWIC results suggest that different aspects of communication are emphasized in onshore and offshore accountant positions. Words relating to literacy and oracy, technology and English tend to be emphasized more in offshore work, whereas words relating to interpersonal skills appear more frequently in onshore jobs. Acknowledging context as an important factor determining the semantic value of 'communication', I summarize in Table 5.6 the different notions identified in the corpus analysis.

I will now analyze in turn how each notion of communication intersects with hiring practices and ideologies in accounting workplaces. Using Fairclough's (2003) critical discourse analysis framework, I explore the dialectical relationship between these entextualized notions of communication and those reified in other recruitment genres, such as the job interview and written examination. I triangulate relevant excerpts from job ads and interview data to examine how communication skills are

Table 5.6 Communication themes identified in accounting job ads

Themes	Offshore job ads	Onshore job ads
Spoken communication	✓	✓
Written communication	✓	✓
Communicating through technology	✓	
Communicating in English	✓	
Communicating relationships		✓

performed and evaluated as a condition for employment. This approach demonstrates how communication is constructed as a site of competition in the selection process.

5.3 Spoken Communication

The textual analysis of online job ads showed a strong semantic link between speaking and the communication required in accounting work. Whether applicants possess this specific skill may be assessed through 'performative moments' (Urciuoli, 2010: 55). A performative moment is an event where social actors demonstrate knowledge and other forms of competence. As an act that allows applicants to talk, interviews administered by workplace gatekeepers constitute prime performative moments. In this section, I explore how the job interview serves as a site for the performance and evaluation of accountants' competence in spoken communication. To do this, I examine accountants' recounts of their job interview experiences.

The interview, as one of the most established job application genres, has been described as part of the 'generic hiring ritual' (Gershon, 2019: 91). This ritual involves applicants preparing documents such as curricula vitae and cover letters. Designated representatives of the workplace then validate applicants' representations of their employable selves by questioning them on details cited in these documents. A successful interview may mean a job offer or an opportunity to progress to the next stage of the hiring process, which could be another interview or a written test.

Structured as an oral question-and-answer test, this recruitment genre highlights the candidate's speaking ability. Accountants' recruitment experiences indicate what employers consider desirable speech.

Excerpt 5.1

Accountant Corina: [There are] different levels of interview. So from HR [Human Resources] (...) once you have passed the interview, you will be referred to the manager, actually it's two managers – associate director and senior director – and once you have passed the interview and then that's the time you will be referred to the client that you will be handling.

The interview is described as a process of communication involving multiple interlocutors, who interact in a hierarchical progression. In this process, applicants repeatedly perform the ritual of answering questions put to them by the gatekeeper/s. Successfully performing the task with the first level of authority (e.g. human resource staff) leads to another speaking test, this time with someone in a higher position (e.g. manager). The series of spoken tests possibly culminates in meeting the client, that is, the representative of the business headquartered overseas that is seeking accounting services offshore, in the Philippines. The immediacy of this event following the Q&A with workplace representatives gives the impression of a seamless connection between the company and its clientele, making the client part of the hiring decision. The early mention of the client in the employment process potentially reflects what Dlaske (2016: 429) described as 'the customer orientation characteristic of the contemporary new economy'. This kind of orientation suggests that workplace decisions, including who to hire and how the hired workers are supposed to speak, is influenced by the client's preferences (Cameron, 2000b).

Besides the structure of the interview, the types of questions fielded also suggest how employers evaluate accountants' oracy.

Excerpt 5.2

Accountant Nadia: (...) they asked me um 'Can you explain the – from what have you remembered at *sa* school *mo kase nga* fresh *grad ka* – what is the *ano* AR cycle, the Accounts Receivable cycle?' So *in-explain* explain *ko kung ano naaalala ko*. Oh my gosh! *Buti may naalala pa ko*.

[(...) they asked me um 'Can you explain the – from what you remember from your school, because you're a fresh graduate – what is the AR cycle, the accounts receivable cycle?' So I explained what I could remember. Oh my gosh! Thankfully I still remembered something.]

Excerpt 5.3

Accountant Fatima: ...*tinanong* [it was asked] if we can communicate confidently to foreigners...

Excerpt 5.4

Accountant Eva: They asked me about my expectations on the job. And they asked me if after audit, it was okay for me to be transferred to general accounting. So that was it.

Excerpt 5.5

Accountant Myrna: (...) *noong ako ang nag-apply*, very *ano siya – 'Ay ikaw yung ano! Kumusta sina* sister? *Ano* offer *sa yo ng* [Company]? *Magkano?' 'Sa* [Company] *mga 14 Ma'am.' 'Siguro dito bigyan kita ng konting* higher (...)' (...) *Tagalog nga yung* interview so *ganun kamusta kamusta lang*.

[(...) when I applied, she was very – 'Oh you're the one! How are the sisters? What did [Company] offer you? How much?' 'In [Company], around 14 [thousand pesos], Ma'am.' 'Maybe here I'll give you a bit higher than that.' (...) The interview was in Tagalog, like just catching up with each other.]

These excerpts underscore the topics discussed in the job interview, ranging from technical knowledge (accounting processes), specific competencies (confidence to communicate with foreigners), practical aspects of the job (job expectations, work assignment, salary offer), to personal matters (hobbies, common social networks). The variety of topics covered in the employment interview represents the differential priority of interviewers. For instance, the technical question described in Excerpt 5.2 was raised by the head of the accounts receivables team, which Accountant Nadia was targeting to join. Meanwhile, inquiries about the applicant's generic skills, personal preferences and social networks – as exemplified in Excerpts 5.3 to 5.5 – were made by human resource personnel. While these details suggest a possible link between question type and interviewer role, Excerpt 5.3 invites an interrogation of the more critical link between the job interview and its ostensible purpose of validating applicants' skills.

Raising a meta-question – such as 'Can you communicate confidently with foreigners?' – allows the applicant to describe her self-assessed ability yet does not actually provide the interviewer with any meaningful evidence of the skill (unless the interviewer is a non-Filipino themselves). This indicates a shift from the priority of obtaining proof of the applicant's work skills to the performance of the recruitment ritual where interviewer and applicant are mutually engaged in the replication of conventions. In this case, the question calls for an affirmative response: 'Yes, I can confidently communicate with foreigners'. Responding in the negative, while possibly more truthful, goes against the convention of self-promotion that is expected of applicants. It may be argued then that this meta-question was framed to provide the applicant the opportunity to demonstrate her knowledge of the interview norms. The focus on soliciting answers that evince self-promotion rather than concrete proof of the required competence depicts the job interview not so much as a skills assessment genre, but as a language game (Blackmore *et al.*, 2017; Roberts, 2013).

Overall, the accountants' recount of their recruitment experiences illustrates Roberts' (2013: 84–85) point that the job interview is 'a potent mix of regulation and standardisation on one hand and relative freedom and relaxation on the other'. Standardization is signaled by technical questions, formal manner of questioning, and the use of English (see Section 5.6). Meanwhile, flexibility is indexed by personal questions, a casual manner, and the use of Filipino, which reflects the notion of Filipino as primarily a rapport language (see also Sections 4.4 and 6.2.2). These standard and flexible practices bring to light the twofold purpose of job interviews: vetting the applicant's skills set and socializing with the candidate whose skills are deemed employable (Dadas, 2018).

That these two distinct ends are linked to an assessment of how well applicants talk highlights the job interview as a site for the commodification of speaking skills. In this commodification site, speaking skills are treated as proxy for accountants' competence and personality and are evaluated based on unarticulated ideologies of good oracy (e.g. English as standard medium for job interviews, see Section 5.6). On their part, applicants navigate the variety of registers used by different figures of authority to demonstrate their work competence and ability to integrate into the workplace (Gershon, 2019). Equally important is their ability to replicate past conventions in order to demonstrate their knowledge of the rules of the language game (Piller, 2016). As Roberts (2013: 91–92) puts it, 'The selection interview requires both bureaucratically processible talk and a vivid social performance, subtly blended together to produce a credible and persuasive self which aligns with the ideal worker in the new capitalist workplace'. This high-stakes assessment of spoken communication is sometimes accompanied by a test of literacy or writing skills.

5.4 Written Communication

Frequently represented as co-occurrent with speaking, the ability to write is another salient aspect of 'communication' in job ads. Writing, like speaking, represents a skill that accounting graduates possess, as literacy and oracy are conditions for a university qualification (see Section 3.3). That job vacancies stipulate it as a requirement begs the question of motivation: Why are employers asking for something that the population of applicants will very likely already have? One way to interrogate the discourse of literacy as a job requirement is by examining the ways in which applicants' writing skills are assessed in the hiring process.

Three writing performative moments that allow the applicant to demonstrate the skill are the curricula vitae, the cover letter and the standardized test. The curricula vitae or CV, also referred to as the résumé, is a text produced by job seekers summarizing their qualifications and skills as employable workers. There appears to be a general understanding of how this text should be presented as it is minimally mentioned in the job ads as a required application document. However, there are more nuanced references to the cover letter and the written tests, which I now discuss in turn.

The cover letter is a written expression of interest in the advertised position. It provides a brief self-introduction of the applicant and refers the employer to the résumé with the hope of being considered for an

Table 5.7 Cover letter as a required text for offshore accountant positions

Framing of cover letter	Excerpts from online job ads
1. Adjunct of CV	Please send your resume and cover letter.
2. Written interview	Cover letter answering these questions: -Short introduction about yourself -What is your future career goal? -How will you contribute on the company's success? -What are your plans to do if you never use QuickBooks before?
3. Incentive	A resume is expected, and a cover letter or proper introduction is a plus! Emails that are sent with a cover letter or a genuine proper introduction will quickly be read first.
4. Condition for rejection	You will be automatically rejected if your cover letter does not: Demonstrate you have watched our slides; and Tell us why you want to work in the health-care industry; and Read without grammar and/or spelling mistakes and errors Nonpersonal (generic) applications will be IGNORED. Irrelevant information in cover letter pertaining to nonrelevant skills and/or not specific to this job will show me that you are not serious, have not read the ad and do not value the position or more importantly yours or our valuable time!

interview. This text is explicitly mentioned and variably constructed in online job ads for offshore positions, as shown in Table 5.7.

As the excerpts indicate, cover letters are a routine text accompanying the CV. It is seen as an indication of applicants' interest in the position. A cover letter that follows given instructions, exhibits grammatical and spelling accuracy, and is tailored to the advertised position is seen as reflecting a serious interest in employment. This kind of letter is linked to promises of priority attention, implying an edge over other applicants. Conversely, noncompliance is associated with negative consequences (rejection, being ignored). The discourse of rewards and punishment in relation to the cover letter demonstrates control of communication skills by linking specific notions of writing (e.g. grammatical accuracy) with employability. Additionally, such discourse may be a way of managing the number of applications sent through. By stipulating specific conditions for the preparation of the text, the employer can filter out candidates who are unable or unwilling to invest time to produce a customized cover letter.

Another recruitment event where accountants can perform their writing skill is the standardized test, which is designed to measure competencies such as general aptitude, attitude, literacy and numeracy. The content and criteria of this written test may vary for each company and position as described by accountants.

In some cases, the written test features items that measure aptitude, attitude, numeracy and grammar knowledge – in the same way that school entrance tests are traditionally purposed.

Excerpt 5.6

Accountant Nadia: (...) *para kang nag-exam*, entrance exam *ng* school. *May* math, *may* psychology test *ganyan, may* English...grammar, more on multiple choice *siyempre, yung ganyan*. Grammar--*ano yung tamang* word? *Tapus tama ba yung* spelling *na 'to*? *Ganyan*.

[(...) it's like sitting an exam, school entrance exam. There's math, psychology test like that, English...grammar, more on multiple choice of course, like that. Grammar--what's the right word? Then, is the spelling right? Like that.]

Excerpt 5.7

Accountant Rosario: (...) *meron pong* essay. *Yung mga* questions *po* like, 'Tell me about yourself. Discuss your favorite movie.' *Yung parang ganun po*.

[(...) there's essay. The questions are like 'Tell me about yourself. Discuss your favorite movie.' Like that.]

These areas of competencies may be given equal or differential weight. For instance, the test may be customized to the targeted position, so that the test for an accounting position focuses on measuring math skills that are deemed most critical for the job. The exam may also resemble academic assessment formats like multiple choice and essay.

In other cases, the job exam is distinguished from its academic parallel by its focus on evaluating practical job skills like the ability to produce work genres as described in the excerpts below.

Excerpt 5.8

Accountant Fatima: (...) not strictly grammar items *na pang* college or *pang* high school *pero* more of how will you reply if you receive this email *parang mga ganon*.

[(...) not strictly grammar items for college or high school level but more of how will you reply if you receive this email, like that.]

Excerpt 5.9

Accountant Alma: (...) *magra-write talaga ako ng* email. *Or meron ding* type *na ganun din pero* instead of email is chat. *Parang*, how would you respond. *Parang ganun*, so *marami siyang scenarios*.

[(...) I will actually write an email. Or there's also a similar type but using chat instead of email. Like, how would you respond? Like that, so there are many scenarios given.]

In sum, the different forms and ways of writing featured in the cover letter and standardized test construct the desired communication skill as both a personal competence evidenced by original compositions (as opposed to scripted expressions in templates) and a generic ability that can be tested and scored based on specific language standards (e.g. grammar and spelling). The latter may be linked to what Heller and Duchêne (2012: 12) described as forms of 'taylorism', that is, the management technique for industrial production that 'seeks to maximize efficiency by breaking down production into a standard sequence of steps'. They argue that applying such an approach to writing 'allows us to think of language [or in this case, writing skill], as something measurable, so that standardized benchmarks can be used in teaching and in the evaluation of communicative competence' (Heller & Duchêne, 2012: 13). Such practice, however, is difficult as language and communication do not lend themselves well to the same mode of regulation that can be applied to mechanical work. Furthermore, 'this difficulty is compounded by the attempt to simultaneously attend to standardization and variability, as service and information providers attempt to speak to niche markets' (Heller & Duchêne, 2012: 12). It is precisely this mix of standardized practices and flexible production that comprises the desired and evaluated literacy of accountants. Recruitment narratives suggest that accountants are expected to exhibit both forms of writing ability, which mirrors the double standard for new economy workers to be both scriptable and flexible, capable of being regulated and exercising autonomy (Cameron, 2000b; Dlaske *et al.*, 2016).

Part of the expectations about accountants' literacy is their ability to demonstrate their writing skills digitally. I now turn to how digital literacy as a form of communicative competence is built into the recruitment process.

5.5 Communicating Through Technology

The requirement for technological literacy in accounting work is highlighted in different stages of the recruitment process. It starts with job ads that repeatedly use technology-related terms such as 'email', 'online', 'internet' or 'virtual'. As mentioned earlier, these terms significantly figured in offshore job vacancies.

The emphasis on technology words in offshore work, however, does not presuppose that onshore jobs do not involve technology. A close reading of the onshore vacancies show that technology is variably referenced as part of the desired qualification, as accounting software and computer applications that are mandatory for the job, as part of the application protocol and as description of the work setting. This variety of references indicates that technology is entrenched across the globalized accounting field, which involves communicating with social actors in geographically dispersed settings. This reality has been further enlarged by the advent of the COVID-19 pandemic in 2020 which normalized working from home.

Geographical dispersion explains the heightened valuing of technology. Communication among physically remote co-workers and completion of tasks are necessarily mediated by technology. Consequently, digital knowledge and material resources are emphasized in accounting roles. These include specific hardware capacities, such as high internet speed and computer processor, and the ability to use identified accounting software, communication technologies and messaging applications. Some companies require that applicants for home-based positions have their own device as a pre-condition for the job (also known as 'bring your own device' or BYOD). This practice potentially facilitates the creation of virtual workspaces that enable organization members to collaborate even as they operate remotely.

Beyond these digital qualifications, technology is also constructed in job ads as digital ways of demonstrating and evaluating communication skills. Applicants are instructed to make a 'video clip that tells us a bit about yourself', to 'include your Skype ID and a link to your resume and Facebook or LinkedIn profile' and to do an 'interview via Skype'. Some adverts also require applicants to complete 'mandatory online job tests', including a standardized English test and a personality profile. One advertisement detailed a virtual pre-test.

Excerpt 5.10

> Create a new Gmail account. The email should include the word 'eagle'. Example of correct email address: eagle78@gmail.com
>
> Create a Google Spreadsheet from that account.
>
> Add 3 columns: Keyword, Search Term, Impressions. Use those as column headers. Make the header row fixed – so even if you scroll down it remains visible.
>
> Go to Amazon and search for 'alarm'. Amazon will provide you with suggestions.
>
> Write the word 'alarm' in the Keyword column. Add all the suggestions to the Search Term column – a new row for each one.
>
> Use https://www.semrush.com/ to find out the search volume for each search term on Google US.
>
> Write the volume for each one in the Impressions column.
>
> Share the spreadsheet with beardmaestro99@gmail.com. Make sure it is editable.
>
> Then also send an email to beardmaestro99@gmail.com with the subject 'Challenge #1 Complete' and in the body of the email mention your name and the link to the spreadsheet.

This test, which is described as the first of 12 progressively difficult 'challenges', ostensibly seeks evidence of applicants' digital skills, including making videos, creating spreadsheets, googling and file sharing. A satisfactory output will then lead to another test, which is presumably more challenging. This series of competence performances resembles the job interview ritual, where the priority of applicants is to create a positive impression in each ritualistic Q&A turn. Characterized by the replication of similar actions to demonstrate authenticity of competence and job-worthiness, it may be argued that this virtual challenge, as well as other online tests and digital documents required by gatekeepers, is an evolving form of digitized recruitment ritual.

The digitization of the recruitment process illustrates how 'technologization alters (discursive) practices' and that such 'recontextualization involves shifts in meaning and materiality away from their previous instantiations' (Iedema & Wodak, 1999: 13). In this case, recontextualization from physical to virtual ways of performing competence causes shifts in the explicit valuing not only of material technological conditions but also of the set of skills tied to specific forms of technology. This adds another layer of expectation, which is captured in the designation of offshore accountants in job titles such as 'virtual accountant' or 'virtual assistant' who is imagined to be flexible enough, in terms of skills and time management, to do various other automated and technology-mediated tasks such as data entry, email management, and phone support, in addition to accounting work. Aligning these practices with Goffman's (1990) concept of performance as impression management and Pennycook's (2004) notion of language performance and identity formation, I propose that the virtual work environment is a kind of stage set up by employers for applicants to perform their competence and identity as employable digital workers, who can embody generic skills (speaking and writing) in disembodied ways.

On this digital stage, accountants perform their writing competence through digital cover letters and online tests. To demonstrate their speaking skills, they may be interviewed via Skype, an internet-based software that provides free video calls, instant messaging and file sharing functions for users across the globe. This practice of using technology instead of face-to-face modality for a recruitment ritual demands that both applicants and recruiters are technologically savvy. This involves, for example, knowing how to make eye contact through the computer camera instead of looking at the image of the other person on the screen (Dadas, 2018). Failing to demonstrate this knowledge in the virtual platform may negatively impact the interviewer's impression of the candidate and potentially affect recruitment decisions. This exemplifies how shifting to technology-dependent interview formats heightens the ambiguity of the bases for evaluation. This problem is illustrated in Offshore Accountant Hilda's narrative of her failed online interview.

Excerpt 5.11

Researcher: Why do you think you were declined the first time?

Accountant Hilda: It's because of my speaking. Yeah *kasi yung nag-i-interview* [because the interviewee] actually is virtual. *Hindi namin siya kilala, hindi namin siya nakikita* [We don't know this person, nor can we see him or her]. So we're thinking that he, she, is just assessing us by the way you speak, and not the way, not by our knowledge.

Accountant Hilda describes the virtual platform as depersonalized. She suspects that this '(dis)embodied job search strategy' (Gist-Mackey, 2018: 1265) devalued her work-relevant knowledge and instead highlighted her speaking skills, which she believes is one of her weaknesses. In other words, the digital stage heightened the focus on her communication ability at the expense of a focus on her technical knowledge as an accountant. This impression offers an example of how in a 'high-pressure situation rife with expectations about communicative style and cues, candidates who do not reflect normative expectations can be penalized for reasons other than their capacity as [accountants]' (Dadas, 2018: n.p.). In her case, Accountant Hilda alleged that she was penalized for her inadequate fluency although, surprisingly, she reported being notified later that she was reconsidered for the job.

The reversal of the hiring decision in turn suggests that while the ability to communicate technologically is emphasized as a criterion for offshore positions, what counts as 'good' communication in a virtual environment and how the assessment of this skill contributes to the final recruitment decision are not always clear. The ambiguity of this hiring criterion is also captured in the following descriptions from two offshore job ads.

Excerpt 5.12

> A lot of work is conducted over the phone or by email so clients need to quickly understand what you are saying.

Excerpt 5.13

> We are looking for punctual, reliable and detail oriented person and well spoken who can communicate well in english via email, video, Skype, facebook messenger that would like to be part of a professional accounting firm that values the clients as first, employees second.

On the surface, these excerpts appear to be centered on the applicants' ability to use communication technology and social media for work purposes. However, woven into these descriptions are references to other desirable qualities, which are both specific and abstract. For instance, phone and email skills are tied to generic notions of 'good communication' such as comprehensibility and English proficiency, as well as other traits linked to corporate professionalism such as punctuality, reliability, detail-orientedness and client-focus. This compounded construction of the employable accountant indicates that the virtual work environment where globalized accounting practice is set is re-shaping the hiring criteria, expanding the idea of the employable accountant as one who is simultaneously professional, communicatively competent and digital.

Overall, the salience of technology as part of the hiring criteria for globalized accountants is rationalized by the need to connect geographically dispersed organization members. As employers restructure hiring practices around the forms of technology used in organizational communication, technology-dependent methods of self-presentation and skills performance seem to shift the focus from the applicants' technical accounting knowledge to their digital communicative skills. Along with this shift is the reconstruction of accountants' identities as virtual workers, who are expected to manage multiple technology-mediated tasks related to accounting or otherwise while simultaneously embodying abstract ideals of a good communicator and corporate professional. The weaving of these concepts in the job ads discourse and the recruitment process makes good technological communication salient yet obscure. What is clear is that to be employed, globalized accountants are required to step on a digital stage – a virtual platform where they have to perform their communication skills, which may potentially be treated as a proxy for their technical knowledge and competence as accounting practitioners. In other words, in a work context where accountants need to work in virtual teams, the hiring decision tends to hinge upon their ability to demonstrate their digital communication skills more than their digital accounting skills.

One aspect of this virtual performance is the use of the prescribed language of the workplace.

5.6 Communicating in English

In terms of language, the desired communicative ability of accountants is strongly linked to proficiency in English. As corroborated in the corpus analysis, English strongly collocates with 'communication' (see Section 5.2.2). Other languages are only occasionally named as part of the job requirement. For instance, one offshore job ad requires proficiency in Thai, Spanish, Mandarin, Japanese or Korean, in addition to English, for an 'Accounting Bilingual Specialist' position, which involves translating between English and one of the other named languages. Another ad specifies, 'Good command in English (French an advantage)'. Yet even in these outlier ads, where proficiency in other languages is mentioned as a requisite or advantage, English is identified as the primary linguistic requirement. The excerpts below show variable ways that English competence is prioritized in job vacancy notices.

Excerpt 5.14

Make phone calls in English, talking to Americans, to complete administrative errands for CEO

Excerpt 5.15

You must speak impeccable English with no discernible accent as you will be talking to clients.

Excerpt 5.16

> Fluent English, we would request a personal letter from the applicant in English to see the level of English together with a C.V.

Excerpt 5.17

> To be considered for this role, applicants should possess the following: MANDATORY ONLINE JOBS TESTS (Must be listed on your profile) English Test result of C1 or C2 (Advanced)

Excerpt 5.18

> Strong written English skills are a major plus, and will influence compensation. Strong oral English skills are another additional plus that can influence compensation as well.

The excerpts indicate that English is the mandatory medium of interaction with specific speakers of English (e.g. Americans) and workplace powerholders such as CEO and clients. Oral proficiency in this language is defined in terms of accent while written proficiency is validated through cover letters and standardized test results. Finally, the ability to show evidence of spoken and written competence in English comes with a promised reward of good compensation.

These variable descriptions of the desired English skill reflect employers' valuing of its utility in the workplace tied to notions of 'fluent', 'advanced', 'impeccable' and 'strong' language skills. One notion links the desired spoken English to the lack of a 'discernible accent' (Excerpt 5.15), which reveals ideologies about certain accents, possibly those that reflect what Lippi-Green (2012: 46) calls 'L2 accent' or the 'breakthrough of native language phonology into the target language'. This ideology is based on the flawed assumption that people can actually speak without any accent, also known as the 'myth of non-accent' (Lippi-Green, 2012: 44), where 'non-accent' is the code for the phonology of native speakers of English. Reflecting on this ideology, 'impeccable English' implies English without phonological traces of another language, like a Filipino/Tagalog accent. This ideal reflects the standard language myth, which limits spoken language variation by indicating a preference for certain varieties (Lippi-Green, 2012), particularly Inner Circle varieties (Kachru, 1992), at the expense of the erasure of a localizable Filipino identity of the speaker.

Another notion of the desired English skill is linked to proficiency certified by a standardized online English test. Reference to the required 'C1 or C2 (Advanced)' results links the mandatory qualification to the Common European Framework of Reference for Languages, which provides descriptors for levels of competency in a given language. In this standardized language mastery scale, C1 and C2 represent a 'proficient user' of English.

Advanced proficiency in English without phonological traces of Filipino is further enlarged with the labels 'major plus' and 'additional plus', which represent the linguistic skill as an advantage in the selection process. The implied advantage relates to the applicant's chance of securing the role and getting a higher pay. Associating English language skill with better work compensation speaks to the power of language as capital, having both symbolic and economic value (Duchêne *et al.*, 2013).

The explicit commodification of this language skill in turn compels applicants to demonstrate their competence through specified recruitment practices. Besides the mandatory English test and application documents, another key moment in the recruitment process for the performance of language proficiency is the job interview. How English figures in this speech task is described by the accountants.

Excerpt 5.19

Accountant Eva: Um as much as possible I answered in English (...) even though the interviewer would sometimes talk to me in Tagalog, I tried my best to speak in English.

Researcher: Why?

Accountant Eva: (...) commonly said that um during an interview you should always speak in English, you should always try to speak in English.

Excerpt 5.20

Accountant Paloma: Straight English, *siyempre. Yan naman ang* SOP [standard operating procedure] *natin di ba? Pag* interview *ka siyempre yung* panel, *pag hindi ka tinatanong ng Tagalog, wag ka sasagot ng Tagalog.*

[Straight English, of course. That's our SOP, isn't it? When you are interviewed by the panel, if you're not asked in Tagalog, don't respond in Tagalog.]

In Excerpts 5.19 and 5.20, the accountants highlight English as the official medium of the job interview. Monolingual English is described as part of the interview protocol, an established practice in the routine screening of potential employees. Deviating from this norm is depicted as an action that may be initiated by the interviewer, however, not by the applicant.

The designation of English language use as SOP in the job interview reflects Bourdieu's concept of doxa, defined as 'a form of practical reasoning gained from social practice and experience, [which] derives from the relatively (or previously) implicit assumptions about how autonomous social fields work and what goes without saying' (Blackmore *et al.*, 2017: 70). That applicants come to a job interview expecting to be addressed in English and prepared to respond in English – even when the interviewer poses some questions in Filipino – speaks to the power of English as the normalized language of recruitment.

The accountant's effort to stick to the SOP is likely motivated by her desire to maintain an image of professionalism that is indexed by the consistent use of English – a discourse deployed by teachers in accounting and business classes (see Sections 4.2.2 and 4.5.1). Lipovsky (2006) analyzes the candidate's demonstration of her ability to use the language of the workplace (English) as a performance of knowledge of the organization's rules (doxa), which in this case is prioritized over accommodating what seems to be rapport work by the interviewer through Tagalog use. Whether the candidate has satisfactorily played by the language rules and performed her verbal fit for the job, however, is a judgment that remains highly subjective and dependent on the interviewer's ideologies of 'good communication'. This opinion is caught in between tensions to prioritize rules versus rapport, and global versus local ways of talking, which in turn can potentially influence the hiring decision. This condition resonates with Roberts' (2013) analogy of the recruitment process as a language game.

The priority of English in this language game is evidenced by job ads and recruitment practices that construct English as the standard language of accounting work, the SOP to which applicants should conform to create impressions of competence. Using the lens of performance, English may be viewed as the ritual language of performance that is both explicitly named and implicitly understood as the language linked to employability in globalized accounting practice. This ideology is further entrenched by the language-profit discourse that melds 'good English' with 'better pay'. What is considered 'good English', however, is only marginally defined in terms of accent and general proficiency descriptors, which bring to the fore ideologies of standardization that privilege native forms of English.

Another aspect of the linguistic capital required of accountants relates to their ability to communicate in respect of interpersonal goals.

5.7 Communicating Relationships

Interpersonal skills, indexed by terms such as 'team/s', 'relationships' and 'teamwork', were identified as a key requirement in job ads. The interpersonal aspects of accounting are differently described in the excerpts below.

Excerpt 5.21

Confident asking questions, sharing ideas, and working collaboratively with US employers and other VAs [virtual accountants] in Philippines

Excerpt 5.22

Maintain a strong client focus by effectively serving client needs and developing productive working relationships with client personnel

Excerpt 5.23

Excellent communication skills in order to drive interactions that build trust and manage expectations with all stakeholders

Excerpt 5.24

Experience in collaborating with teams across geographic locations

These extracts depict the employable accountant as one who can develop a working relationship with both colleagues and clients, whether co-located or remotely situated. Relationship building with these internal and external stakeholders is oriented toward managing work expectations and engendering trust. These critical relational goals are mobilized in a context that is highly dependent on communication technologies to connect individuals who are geographically dispersed and who potentially bring different cultural and linguistic capital into their interactions (see also Section 6.4).

Interpersonal skills as a hiring criterion brings to the fore the link between relational communication and transactional outcomes and the expectation that accountants simultaneously manage both. This aligns with rapport studies in professional contexts that report a 'high degree of crossover between interactional and transactional language' (O'Keeffe *et al.*, 2007: 182) and fluidity between work and nonwork talk in the office (Grossi, 2012). The overlap is constructed in job ads as associated with the pragmatic effect of rapport on effective service, work collaboration and productivity, which are particularly critical in the spatially fragmented and culturally diverse environment of globalized accounting. In this kind of context, 'solid collegial relations and the effective management of interpersonal rapport underpin the development of trust and the social capital essential for knowledge sharing and complexity of doing relational work in multilingual/multicultural settings' (Angouri, 2014: 3).

Applicants' ability to demonstrate interpersonal communication skills is assessed in the job interview which is a site for the initial interaction between applicants and potential relationship partners at work (supervisors and clients). In this introductory meeting, applicants create impressions of trust primarily by responding to questions, which may be mediated digitally (see Section 5.5) and expressed in different languages of the workplace (see Section 5.6). The simultaneous performance of these skills is routinely embedded in the job interview ritual. It has become normal beyond question, so much so that accountants do not perceive the interview as an assessment of communication competence.

Excerpt 5.25

Accountant Eva: ...the interview questions were, on my part, were actually easy. I think they only asked me for my hobbies... Communication, language skills, wasn't that much highlighted during my job interview.

What stands out in Accountant Eva's statement is the invisibility of communication as a criterion in the hiring process. That she did not see the job interview as a site for the evaluation of her communication including interpersonal competence may be in light of the fact that communication skills were not explicitly topicalized. However, as Kerbat-Orecchioni (1992, as translated and cited in Lipovsky, 2006: 1151) claimed, '...even when the content is indisputably informational, the utterances always have a relational value'. The reverse also appears to be true – that relational messages may have transactional value – as demonstrated by the interviewer who appears to orient interpersonally with Accountant Eva in negotiating job expectations.

The social orientation of the interview is also evident in the experience of Accountant Myrna, who experienced being interviewed in Tagalog. In Excerpt 5.5 (see Section 5.3), she said it felt like she was just catching up with an acquaintance. In this case, the activation of their joint network or social capital may explain the interviewer's casual approach, resembling small talk as further signaled by the use of Tagalog. This example illustrates how relational talk in the job interview indicates familiarity and potentially reifies the interview as a ritual or a mere formality that needs to be performed with an already predetermined, 'friendly' outcome.

This is consistent with Lipovsky's (2006) argument that the interview is a social game. It is a test of the applicants' ability to perform a relationship through language that builds rapport and highlights similarities, such as demonstrating shared values. In other words, the success of the interview depends largely on the interviewers' positive opinion of the applicants' self-presentation, which rides largely on how they use language to perform their identity not only as technically competent professionals but also as enthusiastic, cooperative and trustworthy co-workers (Lipovsky, 2008). Such performance may also be viewed as a 'co-construction of a sense of solidarity' aimed at 'managing rapport at the boundary of the organization' (Fletcher, 2017: 79).

That this social performance is sometimes staged on a digital platform (e.g. Skype) compounds the challenge for applicants who may be differentially prepared to communicate relationally to a power holder (employer) in this modality. For example, Accountant Hilda takes issue with the depersonalized nature of the virtual interview (see Excerpt 5.11 in Section 5.5). In her view, the virtual interaction rendered the focus of the assessment ambiguous – is it the way she speaks, her technical knowledge, or how she presents herself virtually that counts more substantially toward a positive performance? This uncertainty may be associated with the different quality of connection afforded by disembodied hiring practices. Indeed, it is easier for some job seekers to make more meaningful 'interpersonal impressions and connections with potential employers' in embodied, face-to-face interviews (Gist-Mackey, 2018).

Overall, the employability of accountants is constructed as also linked to their ability to perform an interpersonal identity at work. This notion is expressed in job ads as contingent on accountants' initiative to ask questions, share ideas, build trust, manage expectations and collaborate digitally across cultural and geographic boundaries. However, in the job interview, interpersonal communication is seen as less an initiative of the candidate than of the employer, who deploys relational talk as an index of familiarity with the candidate, signaling a predetermined hiring outcome, and as a negotiation device in discussing work-related matters such as job expectations and pay. The dual demand for accountants to passively perform rapport in the job interview and to actively perform it on the job makes interpersonal skills both a salient and ambiguous hiring criterion and points to the differential ways the employable accountant is ritualized in job ads and in work gatekeeping interactions.

5.8 Summary

In this chapter, I explored ideologies about what is considered 'good communication' in the liminal phase of recruitment, where accountants showcase their bundle of technical, communication, digital, linguistic and social skills to prove themselves a worthy fit for the advertised position. Corpus and thematic analysis of these texts also revealed language patterns that suggest differential valuing of communication in onshore and offshore positions. Keywords pointing to relational skills marked onshore job ads, whereas terms relating to speaking, writing, technology and English appeared salient in offshore posts. Triangulating corpus findings with interview data on hiring practices, however, indicated that the assessment of candidates' communication skills did not substantially vary relative to onshore and offshore positions but was generally contingent on the performance of recruitment rituals.

The routine performance of their employability as professional accountants is typically done in monolingual English, considered 'SOP' for both spoken and written communication in recruitment genres. The naturalized choice of English as gatekeeping language, coupled with discourses in job ads that link English proficiency to employability and higher salaries, further enlarges its status as the medium of global professional communication. At the recruitment stage, too, English emerges as the 'superstar' language of accounting that it was also found to be in university instruction (see Section 4.3).

Another important finding is the tendency for oral fluency and digital skills to be treated as proxies for applicants' technical knowledge as accountants. It was noted that when the gatekeeping is done virtually, the digital interface has the effect of heightening the focus on applicants' communication skills so that the outcome of the hiring process may hinge more on the employer's opinion of their digital communication skills than their technical ability. Because of this tendency, accounting teachers, students, and job seekers need to be more attentive to evolving forms of digitized recruitment rituals, which may take the form of a set of online tasks designed to pre-validate the candidate's virtual competence and to weed out of the competition those that fail to make a good digital impression. This trend presents an area of concern as the digital recruitment process now has the embedded expectation that applicants already know how to communicate well using digital platforms. However, besides rhetoric in curricular documents on the value of information and communication technology (see Section 3.4.4), there is no evidence from the accounting education data to validate whether and how students are trained to use work communication technologies.

Whereas the communication challenges faced by accountants aspiring for globalized employment have been attributed to 'gaps' in university training (see Section 2.2), the analysis in this chapter demonstrates that this 'gap' discourse is not the whole story. What existing research has not sufficiently acknowledged and which this research brings to light is the multiplicity of ideologies of 'good' communication in the field. While it is true that the communication curriculum is not (and, in fact, cannot be expected to be) fully aligned with professional work practices, matching curricular targets with workplace communication practices is not a panacea. Examining work recruitment, I found no clear-cut definition of 'good' communication. The fluidity and ambiguity of the concept is partly due to the highly intercultural, multilingual and virtual nature of globalized accounting workplaces. This reality has not been emphasized in scholarship that has mostly focused on ideologies linked to English as medium of the selection process and that has examined either jobs ads or hiring practices, but not the two together as interrelated employment events. Therefore, another unique contribution of this present study is tying together these front and back ends of the recruitment process. This approach offers a big picture view of how the job ads' rhetoric of communication as criterion for employment is both translated and contradicted in recruitment rituals. The noted inconsistencies may partially be linked to the public relations role of job ads, designed also to project and protect the good image of the company. With this priority for 'good' image, it is very likely that the communication standards mentioned in job ads do not necessarily reflect what is valued and done on the ground.

How is communication actually shaped in the accounting space? We turn to this next.

6 Communicating in the Accounting Workplace

6.1 Introduction

This chapter moves the sociolinguistic analysis from the gatekeeping stage to the center stage, that is, the actual workspace where professional accounting is done. Exploring what and how communication is predominantly shaped on the accounting work floor, I begin by examining language use in interactions involving social actors with different professional, linguistic and cultural identities (Section 6.2). Then, the focus shifts to the ways that accountants are styled and socialized to communicate at work (Section 6.3). Finally, digitized communication is analyzed as a site for the performance of corporate accountability, efficiency and productivity (Section 6.4). This last section highlights how the increasing technologization of globalized, transnational work is (re)shaping the way accountants perform professional compliance and agency.

6.2 Language Use in Work Interactions

Language use is shaped by context and the ideologies that persist in its ecology. This is exemplified in the recruitment practice positioning English as the standard medium of employment, supported by ideologies linking English to global employability and better pay (see Section 5.6). Whether this practice and view is extended or challenged in workplace interactions is explored through accountants' communication practices on the ground. The variability of these practices is described by onshore accountant Orlando.

Excerpt 6.1

Accountant Orlando: When you are communicating with your colleagues (...) you can use the language that you are most comfortable with, even Bisaya or Filipino. (...) English is not really a requirement although there are some bosses who would prefer you to communicate in English. (...) What is important is you are able to clearly communicate what your thoughts are. But with the bank, that's a different case because you are bringing the name of [the Company]. Remember again it depends on the kind of bank. But in my case since I am quite exposed with the bigger banks, I think you are expected to converse in their language, you know, the business language. (...) We are also expected to have a good command of the language that they are using, which is English.

The excerpt reflects various ideologies about languages spoken in a professional setting, including communication expectations and priorities. Here, English is constructed as a nonmandatory but preferred language particularly by powerholders ('bosses') and the language of big enterprises ('bigger banks'). These notions align with teachers' rhetoric linking English with large, global businesses and Filipino with small-scale, local vendors (see Section 4.5.3). Meanwhile, Philippine languages are identified as the medium of comfortable expression and collegial interaction. Whether English or Philippine languages are used appears to be contingent on shifting priorities to express clearly, accommodate to the language of the client, represent corporate identity, and perform proficiency in English as the language of business. These intersecting views about language choice mirror the superstar-sidekick metaphors in accounting education (see Sections 4.3 and 4.4), where English is linked to performance of competence before powerholders and Filipino, to relational talk. It also brings to the fore different priorities of work communication that shape accountants' decisions on which interactional language to use. In the next sections, I explore the nuances and ideological underpinnings of language use in domains where English and Philippine languages are differentially preferred and in global client talk where English is obligatory.

6.2.1 Domains where English is preferred

Domains in globalized accounting workplaces where English is implicitly and explicitly privileged include spoken interactions with bosses, work presentation and corporate language policy. Each context of language choice is discussed in turn.

First, in spoken interactions, accountants reported deferring to the language of their boss, who in some cases demonstrate partiality for English even if they can also speak Filipino.

Excerpt 6.2

Accountant Stella: (...) we have a boss who always speak in English even if we speak in Tagalog. (...) she's Filipino, a lawyer. She speaks English strictly and whenever she speaks to us, even just an ordinary, she speaks to us in English. I think she's more comfortable with the English language. (...) *Parang* [It's like] I feel inferior if I don't respond to her in English. *Eh* sometimes, I'm not really articulate in English.

Excerpt 6.3

Accountant Nadia: ...more on *Tagalog kami. Kasi* usually *ang mga kausap ko* fellow Filipinos *din. Pero 'pag mga kausap ko mga* boss, *'yon dun ako nag-e-English. 'Pag boss lang.* [...we use more Tagalog because usually the people I talk to are also Filipinos. But when speaking to a boss, that's when I use English. Only for a boss.]

Excerpts 6.2 and 6.3 represent English as both the language used by power-holding social actors and the medium used to address them. This practice is associated with feelings of intimidation and inferiority, what other accountants described as being 'starstruck' or awed by their Filipino superiors who routinely speak in English at work. These attitudes reflect ideologies of superiority and prestige that link the boss's language to high status in the workplace hierarchy, which has the effect of constructing English as an index of power. The notion of power associated with English highlights the power asymmetry between the boss who represents institutionally designated authority and the accountants, whose recognition of their subordinate position conditions them to defer to the language used by authority. This view compels the accountants to follow the boss's language lead to signal knowledge of language rules of politeness, a practice also noted in job interviews (see Section 5.6). The use of English in spoken interactions among vertically oriented Filipino coworkers demonstrates that hidden norms typically follow the pattern of the dominant party's practice (Lippi-Green, 2012).

In addition to being identified as the preferred language of most spoken interactions with superiors, English is also the preferred medium in written professional communication. The most salient form of writing that accountants engaged in, particularly for official external communication, is email (see Section 6.4). Sample emails provided by my participants are predominantly constructed in English with the minimal exception of Filipino politeness markers like *po* and *Ate* (see also Section 4.4) in internal communication. Besides this symbolic use of Filipino for relational talk, the choice of English is markedly consistent regardless of the location and linguistic background of the receiver. Accountants Rosario and Paloma rationalized this language choice as part of a 'standard' that all formal work documentations, that is, written communication, should be rendered in English. This echoes the 'English as SOP' discourse in job interviews (see Section 5.6), where English is constructed as the normalized medium in performing competence.

Excerpt 6.4

Accountant Stella: (...) It's okay to speak also in Tagalog because they [clients] also speak in Tagalog *pero parang mas* authoritative *ka ba kapag* [it's like you're more authoritative] if you deliver your report in English.

Onshore accountant Stella articulates an ideology that rationalizes the designation of English as standard medium for professional communication, that is, the view of English as language of authoritativeness. This perception mirrors the practice of teachers in accounting schools of requiring students to perform knowledge in English by delivering oral presentations and submitting written outputs in what teachers consider the 'superstar' language in the accounting field (see Section 5.3). So far, it is clear that in both accounting work and education settings, English is considered the primary language for the performance of knowledge and competence.

This pattern of language choice is largely taken for granted as 'common practice' among accountants. Using English to perform technical competence is seen as 'normal'. This is probably why formal language policy is not very common in this context. Using English comes so naturally that there is no need to force people to use it. There is, however, an exception in the case of an offshore accounting office I visited.

Boss Tita, a Philippine-born Australian citizen, runs a Manila-based company that provides virtual accounting service to Australia-based clients. Residing in Sydney herself, she would occasionally visit the office site in Metro Manila. One of her anxieties about her Filipino accounting staff is their limited English proficiency, which she says resulted in negative reviews from previous clients. To arrest this communication issue, she believes the solution is to expose accountants to more English by making it the exclusive language at work. She reported replicating the practice from other business process outsourcing companies that purportedly aim to make Filipino employees more comfortable in speaking English, the language of client interactions (more on this in Section 6.2.3). When asked their opinion about the policy, however, accountants appeared far from comfortable with the idea that they are required to speak in English even with their Filipino colleagues. The dissonance in employer and staff views about the corporate language policy is further examined in Section 6.2.2.

This language management practice reflects another way that the power of English is reified, that is, through an explicit imposition on employees' freedom to choose other languages for workplace communication. While this is not unique to the globalized accountant's experience (see e.g. Kirilova & Angouri, 2017; Piller & Lising, 2014), it is problematic because it conflicts with practices and ideologies of local communication, which is a large yet under-researched part of the workplace ecology. This global–local tension, in turn, contributes to the linguistic anxiety of accountants, who are expected to accommodate their language choice to the shifting priorities of workplace communication.

In sum, the predominance of English in spoken interactions with bilingual bosses, in the official written and spoken presentation of work, and in corporate language policy contributes to the construction of English as a language of power. Power here refers to the authority indexed by the boss's institutional status and the force they implicitly and explicitly exert on accountants' language choice. As the subordinate in this vertical work relationship, accountants choose English where it is spoken and imposed by figures of authority, and where they desire to (re)create an impression of authoritativeness in their performance of technical knowledge. These practices and undergirding ideologies about English align with Lüdi's (2017: 349) point that 'a key dimension of...power play [in a multilingual work context] is the choice of language either as it is imposed by the company or negotiated in interaction'. Furthermore, it shows how 'language choice becomes part of the web of relationships and the inherent power (im)balance which brings to the fore the politics of difference relevant [in the] setting' (Angouri, 2014: 4). From these domains of English dominance, I examine next contexts of work interaction where other languages are advantaged.

6.2.2 Domains where Filipino and other Philippine languages are preferred

While English is positioned as the default choice in vertical, formal and external corporate communication, Philippine languages are notably preferred in horizontally oriented, internal work communication. In these interactions, where notions of dominance and subordination are erased, Philippine languages are preferred as medium of consultation and rapport management among coworkers who share the same first language. At the same time, this practice is linked with exclusion and discourtesy by overhearers (Goffman, 1981) who do not speak the language used by conversing parties. How Philippine languages simultaneously serve as medium of inclusion and exclusion, of solidarity and division are discussed in turn.

The most salient use of Filipino and other Philippine languages is in collegial talk. As mentioned in Excerpt 6.1, accountants typically use the language they are 'most comfortable with' in transactional and relational interactions with Filipino coworkers. As medium of transactional talk, these languages are primarily used in consultations with workmates, those back stage dialogs about the work process and reports to be delivered to clients aimed at clarifying and ensuring that the job is done right.

Excerpt 6.5

Accountant Rosario: (...) it [Filipino] is really our language here to make the work easier, when discussing, giving instructions, and reporting, because we're more comfortable with that language and we can easily express ourselves.

Excerpt 6.6

Accountant Paloma: (...) if it's just us, sometimes in our emails, when we ask questions, we use Filipino.

Accountant Rosario's description of the instrumentality of Filipino resonates with the view of all accountant participants, who recognize the value of using a shared mother tongue in managing work-related communication. There is no question that using one's L1 enables ease of expression and comprehension, which is especially important when the content of talk can potentially affect work outcomes.

Besides convenience, the use of a local language is also linked to internal communication. In Excerpt 6.6, Accountant Paloma points to the use of Filipino in emails exchanged among colleagues ('just us'), in contrast with the use of English in external emails (discussed in Section 6.2.1). The insider–outsider distinction is also noted in spoken interactions, such as Accountant Gina's deliberate use of Tagalog when conducting transactions in Philippine government offices, for instance, to physically file tax reports. In this markedly Filipino context, she believes that speaking in English will be frowned upon and possibly taken as an arrogance, highlighting a status differential. Similarly, Accountant Paloma explains that when dealing with rural banks (i.e. banks catering to agricultural businesses and communities located in the countryside), it is common practice to use the local language in the area where the bank is situated. She believes that speaking the same language as the people in the community is a way that accountants can ensure that the locals will not make a fool of them.

These reports suggest that language choice is shaped by the dominant linguistic identity of the institution or community where transactional talk takes place. In these spaces, accountants place a premium on creating a sense of solidarity with their interlocutors, a sense of 'we', of being interpersonally related through a symbolic solidarity of language. They believe that speaking English or a language other than that spoken by the locals has the effect of marking them as outsiders, stigmatized by negative impressions of arrogance and of being a target of deception due to their ignorance of local ways of communication. The opposite premise is that speaking the same local language has the effect of engendering solidarity of purpose and a willingness to cooperate, which potentially makes work easier.

This connection between transactional and relational talk is further illustrated in the excerpt below.

Excerpt 6.7

Accountant Stella: During our meetings with the banks or with our boss, we usually have it in English first, but later on (...) we also do it in Tagalog. (...) *Siguro para maging* relaxed din *siguro ang ano yung* atmosphere *ng* meeting [Maybe in order to make the atmosphere of the meeting more relaxed] (...) When we become familiar *na* [already] with each other... we speak in Tagalog.

English is described as the language of vertical communication (also discussed in Section 6.2.1), which indexes a power differential and is linked to initial impression management. This is contrasted with the use of Tagalog, which is described as the language of familiarity, engendering a positive sense of ease among its speakers as they exchange work-related messages. Here, the shift to Tagalog indicates a more horizontal orientation, which has the effect of incorporating rapport work into work talk.

The intersection between formal and informal work relationships is also seen in the use of small Filipino words ('*po*', '*Ate*') in internal emails (see Section 6.2.1), which index 'patterns of intimacy and equality between management and employees' (Goffman, 1990: 118). These scenarios reflect that in accounting work communication, transactional and relational goals are simultaneously targeted through the purposeful choice of a medium for interaction that strategically (de)emphasizes power differential.

This relationally motivated language choice is less automatic, however, in the case of offshore accountants communicating with conationals overseas. Accountant Alma describes the language choice of her Filipino counterpart based in Sydney.

Excerpt 6.8

Accountant Alma: (…) *nakaka-Tagalog naman sila* although *kapag nandun, sinasabi naman niya na 'Nandito ako sa* workstation, *mag-e-*English *ako.' (…) Pero nung kaya na niya (…) maghanap ng kung anong* space *ang* available *para mag-*talk *kami ng Tagalog.*

[(…) they can speak in Tagalog although she would say 'I'm in my workstation. I'll speak English.' (…) But when she could (…) she'll find another available space so we can talk in Tagalog.]

Highlighted in this excerpt is the effort to find a space where it is safe to speak a shared mother tongue. This practice reflects an extra layer of caution in rapport building among conationals where there are overhearers who do not speak the same first language. To do relational talk in this context, accountants choose their medium of interaction based on the linguistic repertoire of overhearers, lest they be offended by the sound of an unfamiliar language. Undergirding this practice is a concern for the exclusion and discourtesy attributed to the use of a language not understood by those who might overhear the talk (e.g. in Piller & Lising, 2014). This imagined intolerance for the public use of a 'foreign' language stems from the widely 'internalized rule' of politeness to 'speak English in a multilingual space' especially if there are monolingual English speakers within earshot (Torsh, 2012: n.p.). Incidental violations of this rule in the Australian context have been reportedly met with strong disapproval expressed in the extreme form of verbal and physical aggression (Piller, 2016).

This evinces that on one hand, Philippine languages are constructed as index of solidarity anchored on a shared local identity and as instrumental in rapport work. On the other hand, they can also be construed as a device for exclusion and index of discourtesy, potentially engendering disapproval and distrust if used in a space where other speakers do not value it the same way.

This negative view of local language use in workplace communication is also foregrounded in the interrogation of the employer-enforced English-only policy in a virtual accounting company mentioned in Section 6.2.1.

Excerpt 6.9

Accountant Hilda: (…) *nung una kong narinig yan, sabi ko—nasa Pilipinas tayo, wala naman dito yung mga* clients *natin.* So *naiintindihan ko kung nandito yung mga* clients *natin*, if you're speaking with them. But really? *Tayo-tayo lang dito tapus ganun?* And then, since *kaming* team is pure Ilocano (...) *hindi talaga mawala sa amin yun* since *mas na-e-*express *namin ang sarili namin* using the Ilocano language. *Nireklamo lang kasi kami na uhm naging* reason *daw yun, yung pagsasalita namin ng Ilocano, na mag-resign yung isang VA kasi daw* he felt OP, out of place. (…) *Bakit naman sila ma-o-OP? Pero okay, naiintindihan ko rin naman,* so as of the moment, we're trying to speak in Tagalog and English *na lang.*

[(…) the first time I heard of it, I said – we're in the Philippines, the clients are not here. I can understand the need for it if the clients are here, if you're speaking with them. But really? It's just us and then this? And then, since our team is pure Ilocano (...) we can't help it since we can best express ourselves using the Ilocano language. Someone complained that our speaking in Ilocano was the reason that one of the virtual accountants resigned, because he felt OP, out of place. (…) Why would they feel OP? But okay, I get it, so as of the moment, we're trying to speak only in Tagalog and English.]

Excerpt 6.10

Accountant Gina: …here, they speak in dialect. You know their dialect, like Ilocano, yeah, they always…. *Parang sanay na kami.* But then the applicants, *'Ano ba 'to? Ilocano office ba 'to?'* …they [the staff] are always talking in their language… *meron at merong lumalabas.* So… even *hindi kami ang pinag-uusapan parang* try to respect *naman* us *na* please speak in *yung naiintindihan naming.*

[…here, they speak in dialect. You know their dialect, like Ilocano, yeah, they always…It's like we're used to it. But then the applicants, 'What is this? Is this an Ilocano office?' …they are always talking in their language… There's always some Ilocano that comes out. So… even if they're not talking about us, we want them to try to respect us by speaking in a language we understand.]

These excerpts capture tensions in accountants' on-the-ground practices and views related to the language discipline imposed by the company owner. There is expressed consensus on the use of English to communicate with clients (more on this in Section 6.2.3) and the inevitability and ease of using a shared mother tongue. These understandings highlight a tension between creating a global company identity linked to English and of forming a local in-group identity linked to Ilocano. For Ilocano-speakers like Accountant Hilda, speaking this local language shared by her team members makes their work easier. Yet for non-Ilocano-speakers like Accountant Gina, using a local language in the presence of people who do not speak it is excluding, discourteous and potentially damaging to the aspired image of the company. The solution proposed to address the tensions arising from shifting priorities of client and collegial talk, and global and local identity formation is a corporate policy to speak only in English, which however is reportedly implemented as using English and Tagalog in the office.

These reports reflect a dissonance between language policy, ideology and practice. In this case, the dissonance stems from the multiplicity of language concerns targeted by a monolingual policy that purports to make accountants more conversant in English. At the same time, the policy is described as a move to fashion a particular linguistic identity for the office. This aligns with Lüdi's (2017) point that language choices in multilingual workplaces are partly shaped by the corporate identity that the company's management is aspiring to promote. For example, Piller and Takahashi (2013: 114) contend that the English-only policy imposed on Japan-born, Australia-based flight attendants is motivated by a desire to make the airline 'look (or sound) Australian' – comparable to the non-Ilocano identity aspiration held by Boss Tita for her Philippine-based off-shore accounting company catering to Australian clients.

Besides identity construction and impression management, another policy motivation disclosed by Accountants Hilda and Gina is to ban Philippine languages not spoken by all members of the organization, in this case, Ilocano. Attempting to simultaneously meet clients' communication expectations, engineer a nonlocal company identity, and engender solidarity among workmates speaking different L1s results in an ambiguous corporate language policy. This tension reflects Duchêne's (2008: 12) description of language as 'the object of struggle because, at play behind these objectives of homogenization, are ideological stakes and eminently political choices in which languages, varieties and practices will be put into a hierarchy'.

Although hierarchized, Philippine languages are generally preferred in horizontally oriented interactions with conational coworkers. I examine next a domain of workplace communication where language preference is moot.

6.2.3 Medium of global client talk

Communication with global clients is a domain where the medium is preset to English, possibly the client's first language or at least a language spoken by both the client and the offshore accountant. Accountants' interaction with clients is thus predominantly carried out in English for both work and nonwork talk. Small talk is an example of nonwork talk that Filipino accountants and their clients engage in. It is a phatic form of communication about off-task topics aimed at 'support[ing] the transactional processes of the workplace' by 'oil[ing] the wheels of collegiality [and] ...mitigat[ing] power in workplace relationships' (Fletcher, 2017: 85). As a relationally oriented type of interaction with powerholders in the workplace, small talk sits somewhere in between vertical and horizontal communication. In this interaction, accountants reported challenges in using English to build rapport with non-Filipino clients.

Excerpt 6.11

Accountant Divina: They're here *para lang makamusta yung staff.* (...) we go out (...) to spend time with them. (...) somehow nerve-wracking because we have to speak in English. There should be no boring moment (...) *naikuwento ko na buong buhay ko para lang walang* boring (...) my teammates won't speak at all because they might say wrong. (...) it's really like (...) *nakakaubos ng dugo.*

[They're here just to catch up with the staff. (...) we go out (...) to spend time with them. (...) somehow nerve-wracking because we have to speak in English. There should no boring moment (...) I already told my whole life story so they won't be bored (...) my teammates won't speak at all because they might say wrong (...) it's really like (...) bleeding out.]

Excerpt 6.12

Accountant Alma: (...) *pag nandito sila* (...) all of us should speak in English (...) even if just telling a story. *Yun yung mahirap. Minsan pag-tinatranslate mo kasi* in English, *hindi na yun yung dating.* So *pag ganun, sinasabi na lang namin*, 'It's a Filipino joke.' *O kaya ayaw na namin i*-share, 'Never mind.'

[...when the clients are here...all of us should speak in English (...) even if just telling a story. That's the difficult part. Sometimes if you translate in English, it comes out different. So if that's the case, we just say, 'It's a Filipino joke.' Or we'd rather not share it with them, 'Never mind'.]

Excerpt 6.13

Accountant Brando: (...) *parang mahirap mag-construct ng* sentence (...) I have to buffer like a few seconds before I can express my words (...) *sa mga* small talks *lang* but *sa mga* work-related (...) okay *lang.*

[(...) it seems hard to construct sentences (...) I have to buffer like a few seconds before I can express my words (...) only in small talks but in work-related talk... it's okay.]

These excerpts reflect the challenges of using English to do relational talk where interactants do not share the same cultural and linguistic background and where the default medium of interaction is the first language of one but not of the other party. In this context, accountants who speak English as a second language articulate their linguistic insecurities in keeping the conversation flowing, performing humor and demonstrating fluency in social talk with clients who speak English as their mother tongue. The marked asymmetry in their facility of English has the effect of making social talk an anxious activity for accountants to the point of silencing those who fear losing face over their disfluency. Because it is not the language they comfortably use for friendly conversation (see Section 6.2.2), accountants feel coerced rather than engaged to participate as depicted by references to bleeding out, difficulty in translating humor, and delayed language processing and production. Overall, accountants construct small talk in English as a fraught form of relational interaction potentially marked by coercion, silencing and embarrassment.

The language-related challenges in interpersonal client interaction reflect tensions in ideologies about language use in global work contexts. As mentioned earlier, Filipino accountants view English as a predominantly transactional language (see Section 6.2.1) and Philippine languages as primarily relational (see Section 6.2.2). This view, however, is challenged in the context of client interactions, where English is exclusively designated as medium for both transactional and relational conversations. The value placed on maintaining a positive relationship with clients by communicating well in English provides the pretext for explicit language management, such as English-only policy, which may be viewed as a device to extend the scope of English not only as language of formal competence but also of casual camaraderie at work.

This crossing over of English from the transactional to the relational domain of communication is marked as uncomfortable and unnatural, like a form of violence described as 'bleeding out'. This graphic analogy relates to the term 'nosebleed' more typically used by Filipinos partly to describe the linguistic burden, marked by feelings of discomfort, intimidation, embarrassment and panic, when communicating with speakers who are markedly more fluent in English (Osborne, 2018). Used in this context, the linguistic tension likened to physical injury reflects the accountants' view of the incompatibility or abnormality of using a language other than their mother tongue for relational talk situated in the Philippines. Accountants recognize English as the language of global accounting work but feel awkward about using it for nonwork talk in the same context. This sense of unease depicts English as a kind of alien entity invading a space (social talk) that is designated as the province of their mother tongue. Violation of this natural order is marked by signs of being weakened such as the sense of 'bleeding', going silent, responding slower or abandoning speech – 'never mind'. This metaphor dramatically reflects tensions between global and local language ideologies about the practical use and symbolic position of English and Philippine languages in workplace interactions that are oriented vertically, horizontally or somewhere in between.

In sum, social actors in the global accounting workplace carve out spaces in interaction for different languages. English is constructed in interaction as the language of power, global identity and impression management – functions that mirror the 'superstar' language discourse of teachers (see Section 4.3). Meanwhile, Filipino is designated as the language of solidarity, local identity and rapport building, that is, the language for performing 'sidekick' functions (see Section 4.4). These taken-for-granted positions and roles of the two dominant languages, however, are variably negotiated in workplace interactions.

An example is the English-only policy in Boss Tita's company, which, in practice, is implemented as English-and-Tagalog-only in the workplace. This demonstrates how accountants actively negotiate the position of Filipino relative to English and relative to other Philippine languages spoken in the workplace. It reflects a resistance of monolingualism, which heightens their linguistic insecurities. Another way that accountants manage linguistic challenges at work is by taking a less active verbal role when engaged by global clients to do small talk in English, a fraught form of interaction that Filipino accountants describe as life-draining. This tentative participation in small talk also potentially exemplifies what Canagarajah (2000: 122) calls 'false compliance' – a subtle, agentive strategy signaling resistance to the hegemony of English in transactional and relational interactions at work.

Overall, the practices and ideologies that variably intersect in global workplace interactions indicate a hierarchization of languages at work. On this linguistic stage, English and Filipino are positioned front and center, albeit differentially – English, more spotlighted than Filipino. Meanwhile, other Philippine languages (e.g. Bicolano, Bisaya, Cebuano, Ilocano, Ilonggo, Cebuano) are pushed further into the back stage in smaller circles of interaction. Such positioning of language in workplace interaction potentially shapes practices and beliefs as regards language learning at work, which is discussed next.

6.3 Corporate Communication Training

Habitual linguistic preferences and the notion of standard language use in work interactions may be attributed in part to communication training practices in globalized accounting workplaces. In this section, I examine how accountants are socialized to communicate at work and what ideologies are (re)produced in the process.

As regards communication socialization, accountants identified two processes that shape the way they communicate at work, which I refer to as formal and informal training. Formal training pertains to structured, company-organized programs that are delivered by internal or external trainers identified as experts in communication. Where the workshop is externally provided, their completion may involve a training bond agreement, which binds the employee to the business for an agreed period of time to ensure that the skills gained from the training will benefit the company that sponsored it. For example, Accountant Nadia signed a contract to stay with the company for 18 months in exchange for her participation in a 128-hour communication workshop. Breach of this agreement would mean that she would have to pay the company the cost of the training. These seminars are typically delivered in person or in some cases online as part of accountants' mandatory professional development. By contrast, informal training pertains to unstructured, experiential ways of learning communication practices in the company over time. This includes casual mentoring by supervisors and peers and accessing sample reports and emails prepared by more experienced colleagues as guides for text production. Further distinctions between these two forms of training are foregrounded in the excerpts below.

Excerpt 6.14

Accountant Orlando: (...) we term it as soft skills (...) communication in general. (...) We also have business writing course...how to, you know, technical reports in English. (...) It reminds you of the common flaws. It reminds you of the acceptable...best practice or standards and so forth in English construction and conversing.

Excerpt 6.15

Boss Urduja: We do have in-house training but most of our trainings are concentrated with the skills. (...) with regards to their day to day conversation with the client, somehow they are equipping themselves. They are being resourceful enough to improve their skill.

Excerpt 6.16

Accountant Divina: It's up to us (...) Every client is different, how they handle, different attitude so you have to handle them differently. So the company could provide a general but they cannot provide a specific for each client (...) *Sariling diskarte* [our own strategy].

In Excerpt 6.14, formal training is described as a site for norm construction, defining acceptable and flawed ways of communicating at work, legitimizing English as the standard medium of corporate communication, and prescribing specific forms of English as 'best practice'. The two courses that Accountant Orlando referred to focus on meeting and presentation skills and on supervisory writing. Both trainings targeted to accountants in supervisory roles are provided by internal resource persons. The training outlines and handouts indicate that the first course focuses on developing skills in making introductions, interviewing and conducting meetings. Each major section of the five-day training begins with defining expectations and targets for the day's session. This is followed by discussion on identified topics, such as impression management, verbal and nonverbal aspects of presentation, speaking with confidence and building credibility. These topics are variably presented in the form of typologies (e.g. types of handshake), common 'pitfalls', how-to guidelines (e.g. how to 'dress for success'), 'rules to remember' and ways of 'appropriate' self-presentation. The course culminates with individual presentations by accountants in a simulated board meeting with the invited participation of actual senior managers. Presentations are videotaped and played back for peer evaluation. The second course adopts a similar structure in providing input, practice and feedback on corporate report writing. Other topics covered by formal training reported by Accountants Alma, Fatima and Nadia include American English, emailing and intercultural communication. Although varied in focus, these courses are all delivered in English and follow academic patterns of lesson flow, teaching strategies and graded assessments so that Accountant Nadia describes it as '...*parang nasa* school *talaga* [...like we're really in school]'.

Company-organized communication training is contrasted with the practice of holding employees responsible for their own communication skills development. Describing this approach, human resource head Boss Urduja and Accountant Divina (Excerpts 6.15 and 6.16) explain that accountants are expected to improve their ability to communicate at work through individual resourcefulness and strategies to create satisfactory client interactions. Some of the strategies learned and used by accountants to cope with the communication demands of their role are using local languages to do work consultation with conationals (see Section 6.2), shifting from spoken to written channels (see also Section 6.4), seeking the intervention of supervisors or more experienced colleagues and using Google Translate and company-provided templates.

These corporate training processes point to the ways that language ideologies are disseminated in the accounting workplace. One is through the explicit teaching of communication skills, which 'clearly has normative and standardizing effects' with the view to erase variations in interaction (Cameron, 2002: 80) and to (re)shape employees' language and communication practices in ways that are construed as 'appropriate' and 'effective' in the corporate context (Dunn, 2013). Norm construction is evident in the prescriptive language of workshop materials, articulating dos and don'ts, and tips that construct some practices as 'best' and others as 'flawed' albeit sometimes ambiguously. For instance, the training handouts identified 'protecting the corporate image' as one of the 'dos' in introducing members of a team. Maintaining 'good' corporate image is linked to establishing rapport with the client, following the correct sequence of introductions, and observing other 'special procedures' of the team. This exemplifies how accountants' communication practices are styled so that how they speak and write positively reflect on the image of the company (Cameron, 2000b; Dunn, 2013).

Using the lens of performance, formal training may be viewed as a rehearsal or preparation to stage professional communication for the key audience that is the client, whose opinion of the company is valued since it affects the continuity of business. Where such structured rehearsal of idealized communication skills is viewed as an investment that needs to be protected (e.g. through training bond agreements) and as part of the corporate branding effort, communication skills and their performance are commodified as part of the service that clients pay accountants to deliver (see also Cameron, 2000b; Heller & Duchêne, 2012; Urciuoli, 2008).

Besides the explicit styling of accountants' communication practices through formal training, another way that language ideologies are disseminated in the workplace is through rhetoric of agency and autonomy. References to employees' 'resourcefulness' and 'own strategy' echo discourses of neoliberalism, defined as 'a form of governmentality interpellating individuals into a form of selfhood and self-governance grounded on a responsibility to cultivate oneself as a form of human capital or personal enterprise' (Urla, 2019: 266). This reifies a 'culture of self-improvement' (Cameron, 2002: 74), which operates on the assumption that employees will (or should) exercise initiative to 'acquire new skills to cope with new demands and learn from each other as part of their daily routine at work' (Angouri, 2010: 207). Put differently, companies make communication training the accountants' self-initiated project. They are expected to style themselves as they interact with clients and coworkers, adopting modeled ways of speaking and writing over time. In this way, accountants develop experience-informed knowledge in respect of 'real-world' communication, which is constructed as one of the gaps in communication instruction provided by schools (see Section 4.5).

The concomitant use of these two approaches in communication training foregrounds the intersection of authority and autonomy. On one hand, the formal approach imposes norms of 'good' professional communication tailored to the imagined preferences of global clients. On the other hand, the informal approach appeals to accountants' agency to develop skills and strategies tailored to the specific needs and expectations of their assigned clients. Despite differences in approach, both authoritarian and autonomous styling enlarge language and communication as devices for impression management.

In this section, corporate communication training was explored as a site for the (re)production of notions and norms of 'good' professional communication. How these learned rules are enacted or transformed in virtual communication channels is explored next.

6.4 Communicating Through Technology

In the globalized accounting workplace, technology is the material reality that connects globally dispersed workers and sets up a virtual stage on which to perform their competence. This is especially emphasized in offshore accounting work, which is characterized by the absence of colocation among workers who are operating as a team while individually accountable for specific functions in the work process. For Accountant Fatima, this means waiting for workers based in London and the US to send her data on the trades for the day. When the numbers arrive, she reviews them from her home office in Manila and reconciles any discrepancies. If there are issues, she coordinates with the information technology team in India so that she can send the final report back to the head office in London and the US for reporting to clients by the end of the day. This example of heightened interdependencies in this spatially and functionally fragmented work context is replicated daily in globalized accounting practice with implications for the way accountants communicate and how they view communication at work.

Excerpt 6.17

Accountant Corina: The difference now I think is the language barrier. (…) my previous experience with my local client, it is also very easy for me to have an interaction with the client because I can talk to them personally. I can go to them whenever I want and whenever we have a fieldwork. While in an offshoring services, it is more difficult because there's no direct contact. And then they are not seeing what you are doing but I know in myself that I am really working eight hours and sometimes render overtime if needed.

The absence of colocation or the lack of direct, physical contact with the client, as well as with coworkers in the case of home-based accountants, is described as a 'barrier' that makes work interactions more difficult. The challenge highlighted in this excerpt is linked to the absence of face-to-face interaction in offshore work, which makes more salient the spatial fragmentation and lack of visibility among social actors. The fact that other team members or the client cannot 'see' or monitor offshore accountants as they work remotely is seen as engendering doubt and suspicion about whether they are, in fact, using work hours to do actual work. This suspicion is also reflected in an email sent by a client questioning the accuracy of a virtual worker's reported billable hours.

Excerpt 6.18

Hi [Accountant],

We think this invoice must be wrong.

We are definitely not giving you 13 hours + a day of typing (almost certainly less than half this) and there was also a full week during this period that the typist was sick and no typing was done.

We think the previous month is probably wrong as well (...)

Could you please review them both (...)

Kind regards,

[Client]

The accountant responded to this email with a detailed timesheet to assure the client that the billing is 'based on the actual hours of work done only'. The demand for such validation indicates issues of trust, which may be linked to the limited ability of overseas-based clients to corroborate what Philippine-based accountants are actually doing during reported work hours. This foregrounds the challenges of managing impressions in a technologically mediated environment. Although virtual platforms provide a means for geographically dispersed workers to somehow see each other, they also highlight limitations in transparency. This difficulty was articulated by the owner of a virtual accounting company.

Excerpt 6.19

Boss Tita: Because clients cannot see us, one sense, that is sight, is missing. So another sense should compensate, that is, the sense of verbal communication. If this is impaired, it's not going to freaking work!

This employer's strong view aligns with the argument that, as illustrated in Accountant Hilda's online job interview (see Excerpt 5.11 in Section 5.5), the virtual environment emphasizes workers' communication skills, making the features of their verbal expression, such as fluency and accent, more salient than their technical abilities. The heightening of the demand for accountants who can communicate well virtually and the skills deficit discourse perennially echoed by employers like Boss Tita, in turn, potentially exacerbate accountants' linguistic insecurities.

Besides bringing linguistic skills into sharper focus, communication in a virtual work environment is also constructed as being tied to transparency and accountability, which are hallmarks of audit. 'Audit' is a concept that originated in the financial accounting field in the early 1980s to address 'the economy, efficiency and effectiveness of publicly funded activities' (Power, 1994: 2). While it has since extended to other domains, such as higher education, audit has retained the sense of 'principles [and practices] of scrutiny, examination and the passing of judgement' that operate within a 'relationship of power between scrutinizer and observed' (Shore & Wright, 2000: 59). In other words, audit assumes a position of low trust, especially in scenarios 'where accountability can no longer be sustained by informal relations of trust alone' (Power, 1994: 9).

Characterized by spatially dispersed workers who cannot interact face-to-face and who often do not have a shared cultural context, the offshore accounting workplace represents a case where clients and employers are predisposed to assume 'a posture of critical scepticism' and low trust (Shore & Wright, 2000: 80). The interrogation of trust in this context is evidenced by discourses of (lack of) transparency – described by accountants as the condition of 'not seeing' or not being seen – which provides the impetus for 'new norms of conduct and professional behaviour' (Shore & Wright, 2000: 57).

New norms and practices are reflected in the different ways that Web 2.0 technology is used by accountants to compensate for the perceived limited transparency in offshore work. For example, accountants use cloud-based tools to communicate with other members of the virtual team working remotely. Offshore Accountants Divina and Brando reported using project management applications such as *Basecamp* and *Karbon*, which are designed for virtual workers to 'see + manage everything... (even though they're apart)' (https://basecamp.com/) and to 'manage workflows, communicate with teams and deliver exceptional client work – from anywhere' (https://karbonhq.com/). Using the online tool features, accountants document and monitor their own and other team members' daily productivity.

Communicating through technology is also done by accountants through various internet-based spoken and written communication channels. Table 6.1 summarizes the affordances and limitations of these work communication technologies according to accountants.

Accountants value spoken channels for real-time communication, which enables immediate feedback, as well as faster exchange of information and decision making. The multimodality of video conferencing software such as Skype and Zoom also enables interactants to simultaneously exchange information through audio and video messaging, public and private chatting, and screen sharing. The immediacy of feedback, nonverbal cues and multimodal features of these channels approximate the face-to-face encounter, giving accountants a sense that the interaction is more authentic and creating a stronger impression of connectedness and rapport.

This sense of connectedness is achieved, for instance, in 'virtual team huddles' or video calls where accountants and their coworkers stationed in other geographical locations can discuss work or simply check in on

Table 6.1 Advantages and disadvantages of digital channels

	Digital spoken channels (e.g. Skype, Zoom)	**Digital written channels (e.g. email, messaging apps)**
Pros	Synchronous communication Immediate feedback, faster decision making Nonverbal cues (facial expression, tone) Multimodality (video, chat, screen sharing) Stronger sense of connectedness	Asynchronous communication Flexible response time Recorded messages Exchange of accurate and detailed information
Cons	Pressure to respond instantaneously Difficulty comprehending the accent of some speakers	Delayed response (e.g. due to time difference) or nonresponsiveness of addressee

each other. Offshore Accountant Brando's communication activity log shows a daily Zoom video call with other overseas-based team members and client, where they discuss the team's work progress reflected in the task management system. Accountant Alma also recalls being part of these 'daily huddles' where up to 20 team members from Sydney and different parts of the Philippines would discuss over video call the assigned work for the day. However, since she was given a new role, Alma was removed from the huddle list, which she says made her feel alone. This intimation reflects the value of 'virtual huddles' as a way to cope with the sense of isolation and loneliness that may accompany working remotely for an extended period of time. As home-based Accountants Alma and Fatima described, regular video calls with teammates help them cope with the boredom of working alone at home, where the environment can get too quiet, lonely and boring compared with the more dynamic, embodied socialization in an office setting.

One important disadvantage of digital spoken channels, however, is the pressure to respond right away. As a result, some accountants confessed saying 'yes' when asked if they understood the instructions given via video or audio call even if, in fact, they did not fully comprehend the message. This misrepresentation of understanding potentially has critical implications to the work outcome but is reportedly managed by seeking the intervention of more approachable members of the team after the call. A specific difficulty that was repeatedly mentioned by offshore accountants is understanding the accent of other speakers of English. Accountants Vangie and Gina said that the way they manage this is by asking the person with the 'difficult accent' to email or send them an online message instead. Shifting from spoken to written channels is a strategy to ensure that information is accurately exchanged.

Besides allowing the exchange of accurate and detailed information, another attraction of written channels is asynchronous communication, which means accountants can respond in their own time. There is less pressure to respond right away so they can take their time to read and understand, even seek assistance from other team members or use templates to produce more polished and precise responses. Written channels also provide an instant record of the communication, which is important for tasks that require documentation, such as submission of completed work. The most commonly used channel for this purpose is email, as indicated in accountants' communication activity logs.

While providing these advantages, asynchronous communication also has limitations. Flexibility of response time could mean delays, possibly due to time zone difference or due to nonresponsiveness of addressees, which can be interpreted as inefficiency. To manage delays in a geographically dispersed work setup, offshore accountants have developed virtual surveillance practices that push their overseas counterparts to deliver. Accountants Alma and Fatima describe these digital communication strategies below.

Excerpt 6.20

Accountant Alma: (...) *pag* offshore *kasi lalo ganito naka* work from home *tapus ang kailangan mo is yung* boss *mo na nasa ibang* location, *kung hindi sila* responsive *sa* chat, *parang kasi hindi mo alam kung anong nagyayari sa kanila dun e. Hindi naman nila madalas sabihin na 'O meron muna kaming* party' or '*Meron muna akong* meeting.' *Hindi naman ganun. So yun minsan yung pag*-chase, like *kung nababasa ba niya or sobrang* busy *ba niya*? Unlike *kapag nandito yung ka*-deal *mo or pag nasa* office set-up *ka, madali kang maka-kalabit ng tao.*

[(...) when offshore, especially when working from home, and you need to talk to your boss who's in a different location. If they're not responsive in the chat, you don't know what's going on there. They rarely tell you, for example, 'We're just having a party now' or 'I have a meeting now.' It's not like that. So that's when you chase, like to find out if they've read your message or if they're too busy. Unlike if the person you're dealing with is in the same physical space or in an office set-up, you can easily tap the person.]

Excerpt 6.21

Accountant Fatima: There is first level, second level, and third level escalation. So *kapag depende kase sa* issue *kapag* if it's very critical that it needs to be resolved within the day, *kapag* one hour *hindi ka pa pinapansin,* you escalate it in the first level. (...) So *i*-email *mo yung taong ayaw gumalaw tapos i-cc mo yung* boss *niya at tsaka* boss *mo*. (...) *Pag ayaw pa rin niyang gumalaw* (...) you call the boss of that person and then *sabihin mo na ganito ganyan. Yung* second level, *yung* boss *ng* boss *niya ang naka-cc na. Tapus yung* third level escalation, *yun na mag*-email *na yung* boss *mo sa* boss *niya.*

[There is first level, second level, and third level escalation. It depends on the issue. If it's very critical that it needs to be resolved within the day, if the person does not respond to you within an hour, you escalate it in the first level. (...) So you email the person who does not want to move and cc their boss and your boss (...) If still refusing to move (...) you call their boss and then explain the situation. In the second level, you cc the boss of that person's boss. Then, in the third escalation, your boss will email that person's boss.]

Chasing and escalating are motivated by efficiency goals in a virtual work environment. Chasing is the virtual act of running after someone who appears to be evading an initiated communication, and escalating is the virtual act of reporting a project issue (due to a team member's inaction) to higher positioned individual in the workplace structure. These practices, although potentially effective in achieving transactional goals, could put accountants in a bad light. For example, Accountant Divina narrated that a client once directly escalated the team she was supervising to their company's chief executive officer. The breach of escalation protocols, in this case, tarnished the boss's impression of the accountant's competence, which is tied to a time-stamped measure of productivity.

Applying here the lens of audit, I propose that the norms and protocols for corporate online communication practiced by accountants may be viewed as ways to increase the transparency of remote workers' efficiency, that is, as virtual 'rituals of verification' (Strathern, 2000: 3). For instance, 'chasing' and 'escalating' reflect the language of efficiency by sanctioning the reporting of nonresponsiveness to online communication. These negative reports in turn have potential negative implications on the performance evaluation of the team member, who is constructed as engaging in the indecorous behavior of 'having a party' (Excerpt 6.20) or intentionally 'not want[ing] to move' (Excerpt 6.21), both of which are representations of unprofessionalism.

Using the audit lens, chasing and escalating, as well as the use of workflow management software and regular virtual team huddles, may be seen as controls set up by management to remind accountants that, despite working remotely, they are under constant, even stricter surveillance. Their performance, reflected in their manner and frequency of communication, is closely scrutinized and monitored, engendering anxiety and insecurity on their part (Shore & Wright, 2000). In other words, the protocols of virtual work communication keep offshore accountants on their toes, creating the feeling that they have to constantly measure up to digitized standards of 'good communication' to earn the client's trust, keeping them from feeling secure even in a home-based work environment.

Controlling accountants into feeling insecure about their virtual communication skills, which are treated by powerholders as proxy for their technical ability and employability (see Section 5.5), challenges the idea of autonomy and flexibility (Shore & Wright, 2000) linked to working remotely. This control-flexibility tension is an important issue affecting particularly working mothers like Accountants Alma and Stella, who confessed to being enticed into home-based accounting practice, which they imagined as having more flexibility and independence. Eventually, however, they discovered that the expected autonomy is significantly constrained by digital conditions of surveillance.

In sum, this analysis demonstrates the affordances and challenges brought about by the increasing technologization of professional communication. As accountants' experiences show, communication technologies are an important resource in globalized, transnational work, enabling professionals working remotely to engage in long-distance, virtual collaborations. However, the digital staging of communication creates new forms of barriers in the organization, such as the tendency for heightened distrust and fixation with monitoring productivity and efficiency. In this context, participating in virtual rituals of surveillance and performing competence through strategic use of digital channels may become a priority of professional communication.

6.5 Summary

This chapter examined how communication is tied to accountants' performance of their professional roles onshore and offshore. In the work context, ideologies of 'effective communication' are reflected in social actors' language use in interactions, in corporate training, and in the use of technology for communication purposes.

The findings highlight three key points about professional communication grounded on Global South accountants' experience. First, languages are hierarchized in vertical and horizontal interactions. English, Filipino and other Philippine languages are differentially valued in the performance of authority versus solidarity, global corporate identity versus local affiliation, and deference to overhearers versus preference for social talk in one's L1. Second, the privileged status of English in work interactions, which is already entrenched in the field, is reproduced in company-organized communication training as part of corporate branding. Meanwhile, creating impressions of trustworthiness, productivity and efficiency for various audiences, such as clients, team leaders or teammates, through linguistic and digital strategies, is constructed as both an organizational effort and a personal project of accountants. Third, accountants participate in front-stage language games and digital rituals of work surveillance while exercising strategies of agency back stage.

This final analysis chapter clearly demonstrates the benefit of concurrently exploring the interrelated domains of education and profession. While extant studies have tended toward selectively focusing on either school or employment settings, this research has traced (dis)continuities in the way communication is performed and viewed by social actors in both university and work sites. Noted continuities between the two domains include the hierarchization of languages and the formal styling of communication habits and (re)production of center-English-centric ideologies through explicit language policy and company-organized corporate training. Meanwhile, an important discontinuity between school- and work-situated ideologies of 'good' communication is related to the use of communication technologies to perform competence, transparency, accountability and efficiency in a geographically dispersed and highly interdependent work environment. This aspect of global work communication is glaringly absent in the academic discourse, with potential implications for curricular innovation. Overall, what constitutes idealized professional communication in globalized accounting is diverse and fluid, making accountants' communication work complex yet largely invisible and therefore easily taken for granted.

Now uncovered, the hidden language work of professional number crunchers presents important opportunities for supportive response from both the academia and the workplace. One way is for teachers and work supervisors to acknowledge the reality of multilingualism and heightened digitization in the globalized workplace. Practitioner-teachers are especially well-positioned to shape how accounting students imagine the linguistic ecology of their target workplace. This reality check can inspire curricular and personal initiatives to develop proficiencies not only in English but also in other languages and in the use of digital channels for work communication.

It is equally important to educate members of the accounting field (students, teachers, employers, accountants) on the power of language ideologies to shape communication practices. Being aware that particular views of language influence decisions on when, where and how to use them can empower them to see themselves as agentive language users rather than blind norm followers.

These steps could be a start to unravel the 'poor communicators' tag on accountants and to move closer to a sociolinguistic understanding of what constitutes 'good communication' in this field.

7 What Counts as 'Good Communication'

This research reexamined the view of accountants as 'poor communicators' – an occupational stereotype that appears to have the effect of a self-fulfilling prophecy, as accounting education studies have amassed evidence supporting this negative typecast. Set against this background, I investigated practices and ideologies of communication that permeate the accounting field. I began with higher education, the socially ratified site for the (re)production of communication skills. From there I moved on to globalized accounting workplaces, where communication is enacted and evaluated against certain standards of 'effectiveness'. Opening up the dominant and different notions of 'effective' communication in this field is an important initial step in challenging the popularly negative evaluation of accountants' ability to communicate. In this final chapter, I synthesize understandings of 'good communication' in the inter-related domains of education and work in the global accounting field (Sections 7.1 and 7.2). I also discuss practical and theoretical implications for accounting education and sociolinguistic scholarship (Sections 7.3 and 7.4).

7.1 Educating Future Accountants to Communicate Effectively

In schools, where students are shaped into their future accountant selves, communication is typically positioned as a component and outcome of general education, particularly in language units. Comparing old and new curricular documents, however, showed that it has increasingly become part of the teaching and learning plan in accounting and business courses. Developing students' communicative competence is no longer viewed as the exclusive concern of general education, but as an outcome targeted across all components of the accounting curriculum. Besides this, the target communication competence is strongly linked in curricular documents to the global, professional context. This language pattern enlarges the view of communication as an important capital for employment. It also reflects the neoliberal orientation of higher education, which highlights the function of formal pedagogy as a means to achieve employment goals and economic gains.

Examining government, program and unit documents also showed that the desired communication ability is quite loosely defined. It is variably linked to interpersonal skills, spoken and written communication, digital literacy or the ability to use communication technologies, and language proficiency deployed in the contexts of academia, the profession and other domains vaguely referred to as 'real life' or 'real world'. Particularly salient is the connection made between specific languages and participation in the global field. Discourses of globalization largely recognize English as the lingua franca of business in general and of accountancy in particular. Meanwhile, curricular innovations indicate an attempt to negotiate a place for Filipino in this context. Filipino language units were introduced in the 2018 curriculum campaign for the use and symbolic value of Filipino in academic and professional communication, reflecting not only personal competence but also national and global progress and identity. This rhetoric contributes to the symbolic valuing of Filipino as index of nationalism, extending its proposed value in the context of globalization, which was formerly depicted in the old curriculum as the exclusive domain of English.

Taken together, these discursive constructions of communication reflect generic understandings of its instrumental value in achieving transactional and relational goals, the need to adapt communication practices to conditions of the new economy, and the differential valuing of languages as symbolic and economic capital. In sum, the analysis of accounting curricular documents revealed a complex rhetoric about communication, which complicates decisions about actual communication training.

In the accounting classroom, interactional data gave a glimpse of how language and communication practices are shaped by several factors. One factor is the nature of the unit (language- or content-focused). Another is the assigned faculty's ideologies about languages and their value in students' present learning of academic content and preparation for their imagined future workplace. Teachers' opinions and practices indicate a preference for English to prepare students for professional communication and mixing Filipino to facilitate comprehension and attainment of academic goals.

Further probing the language work involved in pedagogy shows that classroom communication entails demonstrating technical knowledge and establishing rapport, which, while concurrently targeted, are ideologically linked to different languages. The 'superstar' and 'sidekick' metaphor aptly captured the hierarchical relationship between English and Filipino – the languages of classroom interaction that alternately take center stage in the performance of accounting knowledge and interpersonal relationship. In this hierarchy of languages, English is largely recognized as the language of accounting as represented by its normative use in reference materials and tests, especially the certified public accountant (CPA) licensure exam, and its prescription as the language of class lectures, student presentations and graded assessments. Whereas English is strongly associated with professional knowledge, Filipino provides a linguistic 'personal touch'. Using this language of interpersonal relationship is seen as having an effect on the perception of the quality of instruction and instructor. Teachers who shift to Filipino to engage with students in a friendly manner, provide verbal assurances and demonstrate an interest in students' personal opinions are favorably perceived by students as 'very effective' communicators.

Another factor contributing to language and communication practices and ideologies in the classroom is teacher authority, which, while traditionally derived from academic qualifications, is also linked to practitioner status. Having occupation-informed knowledge of globalized accounting work, practitioner teachers leverage their 'real-world' knowledge to support their prescription of specific communication practices. 'Real world' here means 'on-the-ground' experience in the accounting profession in contrast to what is dismissed as purely academic or textbook-based knowledge represented by an MA or PhD degree. Work experience as an accountant, especially in a globalized setting where students imagine their future employment, represents an important capital that enables practitioner teachers to position themselves as 'real experts' on what counts as 'effective' written and spoken communication. By extension, this way of thinking distinguishes insider status in the accounting field as representing a superior type of knowledge that somewhat devalues language teachers' expertise, even if PhD credentialed.

The value differentially ascribed to languages and teacher knowledge in accounting education reflects a neoliberal orientation, which, as also seen in curricular rhetoric, constructs higher education as a site for the production of skills that have a potentially high exchange value in the new economy. The future-oriented language practices and the self-view of practitioner teachers as authority on matters of communicative competence indicate priority placed on the (re)production of skills, language habits and ideologies that are represented as valuable in globalized accounting workplaces. These sites are predominantly imagined as populated by 'foreigners' where even Filipino-speaking partners speak exclusively in English and expect accounting staff to do the same.

Overall, I found that although the value of English and Filipino are largely represented in policy as exclusive to specific units (Filipino as exclusive to Filipino language units and English being the default option for all other units), they are actually concurrently valued by teachers and students in classroom interactions regardless of the nature of the course. Even in classes where teachers enforce an English-only policy, Filipino plays 'sidekick' roles in rapport work and in filling linguistic gaps in content delivery and comprehension. This suggests that the monolingual habitus of language policy, which is motivated largely by the imagined hegemonic status of English in the target workplace, is subordinated to the interpersonal and pragmatic value of bilingualism in classroom learning. English, however, is cast as the 'superstar' language of accounting, the automatic choice in performing technical knowledge in the classroom with a view to the transference of this linguistic performance in the work context.

While this linguistic and contextual valuing of communication is foregrounded both in policy and classroom practice, other notions of communication identified from curricular texts were marginally observed in interactional data. Digital literacy, which is highlighted in curricular texts as an aspect of 'effective' communication, was not topicalized nor explicitly taught in the observed classes. The same is true of interpersonal communication, which was not observably emphasized in instruction. These discontinuities between written discourses of communication and interactionally enacted ones represent a 'gap' between theoretical and practical views of communication, which has been represented in literature as an inadequacy on the part of higher education. I argue, however, that discontinuities between prescribed and actual communication practices are inevitable where multiple language and communication ideologies intersect in the context of higher education. Tensions between present pedagogical and future employment goals, between symbolic and instrumental valuing of languages in the classroom and in the imagined accounting workplaces, and between academic and practitioner knowledge of 'effective' communication means that the priority of notions is constantly shifting.

7.2 Performing 'Good Communication' in the Globalized Workplace

In the work domain, I investigated the notion of 'good' communication from the recruitment phase to actual workplace interactions. In the first instance, textual analysis of online job ads demonstrated that 'communication' is widely considered a key employability criterion. The ability to speak, write, use communication technologies, demonstrate fluency in English and do relational talk are frequently mentioned as required communication skills. Although ubiquitous in these recruitment texts, communication skills are also vague as they mostly refer to generic notions that are broadly relevant in the workplace. The ambiguity of this loaded hiring criterion is further reflected in accountants' stories of their recruitment experiences, which emphasized their view of various tests as ritual practices that are routinely observed to mark the transitioning into official insider status in in the workplace. They described how their communication skills are variably positioned as a main feature of the recruitment ritual.

In this veritable rite of passage, accountants' ability to speak is highlighted in the job interview. Central to this semi-structured conversation is the candidate's performance of fluency in English and interpersonal skills, where the relational dimension – signaled by a shift to Filipino or casual talk – is initiated by the interviewer. The normative mobilization of applicants' linguistic repertoires constructs the interview as a language game. Part of the 'SOP' – what Bourdieu (1990) calls 'the rules of the game' – is using English as the assumed medium of the interview and answering questions in a manner that would create a positive impression (albeit not necessarily concrete representation) of applicants' abilities. The priority placed on creating a positive image is linked to the nature of the selection interview as being on some level a social game traditionally done face-to-face. Where this multilingual performance of knowledge and social capital is staged digitally, the recontextualization shifts the valuing of applicants' skills. Shifting from face-to-face to online mode turns the job interview into a digital language performance, which heightens the ambiguity of the hiring decision-making process. Outcomes of Skype interviews, in the view of accountants, are less predictable as the technology-dependent format tends to foreground their ability to communicate online more than their technical ability and knowledge as accountants.

The foregrounding of digital literacy is also salient in written tests that require applicants to compose emails or chat messages for hypothetical corporate situations. This type of assessment, which is contingent on applicants' familiarity with digital written genres, tends to be viewed as more pragmatic, more 'real world' in contrast to other written tests that resemble the academic ritual of the university entrance test featuring English grammar and essay-type items. Although seen as less pragmatic, the use of traditional written assessments as gatekeeping tools suggests a connection between literacy ideologies and practices in academia and the workplace, and the relevance of writing and composition lessons typically provided through language units in the general education curriculum. A rubric of literacy anchored on correct grammar, spelling and format is also used in the preparation of CVs and cover letters. These routine recruitment texts are described in job ads as a test of compliance with language conventions and a demonstration of genuine (as opposed to generic) interest in the position. This construction of standard and customized writing is linked to discourses of rewards (priority attention) and punishment (ignoring, rejection), which foregrounds language control typical in the gatekeeping phase. This discursive strategy points to the value routinely ascribed to communication in recruitment even for positions where language skills are not patently highlighted in the job, such as accounting (in contrast to call center work, for example). That CVs and cover letters are not highlighted in the accountants' narratives, however, indicates the tendency for language control embedded in these texts to be taken for granted as unremarkable.

Overall, the written and spoken recruitment practices and ideologies highlight the ritualized use of communication skills as an ambiguous yet powerful hiring criterion for globalized accountant positions. The digitization of the recruitment process – a necessary innovation in the highly technology-dependent global industry – brings communicative ability into sharper focus so that it can be given more weight than other key hiring criteria, such as technical knowledge and skill. Meanwhile, inside globalized accounting workplaces, the value ascribed to different notions of communication shifts relative to institutional, client and personal ideologies of 'effective' work communication. Observations and logs of work routines and accountants' views about them position communication in between ideologies of authority and autonomy.

The control-agency tension is evident in language choice practices, which are shaped by the pragmatic and symbolic value of English, Tagalog and other Philippine languages in corporate work contexts. Predominantly recognized as the language of power, authority, global business identity and technical competence, English is positioned as the default front-stage medium for interactions with powerholders (clients and bosses) and for official work documentation, especially those externally communicated via email. This view resonates with the 'English as SOP' discourse in the gatekeeping process. Meanwhile, Tagalog is designated in work interactions as the language of rapport, consultative talk with conationals in the office, and local identity – which are typically performed back stage, away from the hearing of non-Tagalog speakers who may otherwise feel excluded or offended by the local language. Deference to overhearers and a concern for maintaining a global (or at least a nonlocal) image push other Philippine languages. Ilocano, for example, is pushed further back stage for relational talk and identity work of a smaller circle of local speakers at work.

While this hierarchical view and de facto use of languages predominantly govern language use at work, the data also shows evidence of what Canagarajah (2000: 122) termed 'false compliance', those 'half-hearted acts' of submission to institutionalized regulation of communication. An example of linguistic acquiescence is accountants' decision to take a passive role in small talk in English with overseas clients. Although not done by all and typically attributed to linguistic insecurity, the choice to be minimally engaged in small talk in English may also be viewed as an exercise of agency, an attempt – however small and subtle – to carve a space of agency in this work interaction where there is no choice but to use English. The agentive view of this passive action is supported by accountants' discourse that compares relational talk in English to something that makes them 'bleed out' – a metaphorical violence against their natural tendency to prefer a more comfortable, more natural language of rapport.

Where there is a possibility to choose the medium of relational talk, that is, in interactions with conational colleagues, accountants' agency is more striking. This is evident in accountants' resistance to a corporate English-only policy. Questioning the necessity to speak in English even with conationals in the office where there are no Anglophone clients present – that is, no audience to perform a global identity to by speaking in English – accountants take corporate language policy into their own hands, revising the English-only policy into an English-and-Tagalog policy. This bold move, albeit not enacted during office visits of the overseas-based employer, reflects an agentive stance against extending the obligatory use of English to relational talk, which is typically demarcated as a Tagalog, backstage domain.

The simultaneousness of control and agency is also reflected in the way accountants are socialized to communicate at work. This is done formally through mandatory, company-organized seminars, and informally through accountants' self-discovery and initiative to figure out what communication strategies work on the ground. Another factor influencing how accountants communicate on the job is the use of technology, which is particularly emphasized in remote work arrangements. On one hand, the virtual work environment gives the impression of autonomy (especially for home-based roles) – that accountants are free to make decisions about how they communicate through various internet-based written and spoken channels. On the other hand, the disembodied and depersonalized modality renders digital communication suspicious, engendering low trust and, therefore, rationalizing stricter surveillance practices. Institutionalized auditing rituals take the form of project management applications that document virtual workers' daily progress, virtual team huddles that are constructed as relationally motivated but are in fact more transactionally oriented, and the efficiency protocols of chasing and escalating.

In summary, the globalized accounting workplace constructs communication as a powerful criterion for employment. It is superficially disambiguated in job ads but increasingly obscured in the recruitment process and in on-the-job interactions. The obscurity of the communication ideal is traced to the intersection of multiple and shifting notions of 'effectiveness' that vary relative to social factors. While doing their technical work, accountants are constantly making decisions about performing a corporate identity linked to the global, transactional use of English and a local identity linked to the local, relational use of Tagalog and other Philippine languages. They also routinely participate in ritualized structures of skills validation, language control and work surveillance in order to be seen as employable, trustworthy and efficient virtual workers. At the same time, they preserve some measure of autonomy by selectively exercising agency in backstage spaces.

What I construe as agentive practices – such as the deliberate avoidance of small talk in English with clients and the revision of monolingual English into a bilingual policy – institutional bosses tend to see as an impairment, something that needs to be rectified. This tendency to take a deficit view of accountants' communication skills shows that the 'poor communicators' stereotype partially stems from a limited understanding of the complex ideological underpinnings of the day-to-day communication work of globalized accountants. One thing that appears taken for granted is the ideological consequences of the increasing technologization and disembodiment of work communication, which engenders trust issues. The low trust toward offshore accountants challenges them to communicate productivity and efficiency. At the same time, it rationalizes heightened surveillance of their work performance, evaluated based on multiple and shifting standards of 'good'.

Collectively, the (dis)connections between communication practices and ideologies across accounting education and work domains uncovered in my study open up important opportunities for accounting and sociolinguistics.

7.3 Adding Value to Communication Training: Implications for Accounting

One important contribution of this study in the accounting field is the foregrounding of communication ideologies as an important shaper of how accountants teach, learn and do communication both in school and in the workplace. What accounting students, teachers, employers, clients and practitioners believe about language contribute in some and different ways to what is considered 'good communication'. Consequently, these beliefs also partly determine who then is judged as 'poor communicators'.

This problematic stereotype of accountants has been largely perpetuated by existing literature. Using sociolinguistic lenses this time, I argue that – as in all stereotypes – what is 'good' and 'poor' are social constructs. What counts as 'good communication' or a 'good communicator' is 'always a socially situated matter, which will always be evaluated within specific relations of power' (Park, 2011: 444). This highlights the need to caution against treating such labels as fact and, instead, to interrogate whose idea of 'effectiveness' is being considered, where and how this idea is deployed, to whom, and for what reasons.

As this study has found, the answers to these questions are not simple and straightforward. One notion in accounting schools is that effective communication instruction mirrors practices in the profession. The desire to match the curriculum with the target profession of the accountancy is undoubtedly important to prepare graduates to enter the profession. However, it is not a panacea to the employability challenges faced by accounting graduates. Neither is it easily achievable. With the continuously shifting notions of 'good communication', updating the accounting curriculum to match an elusive ideal does not guarantee that accounting graduates will ever fully satisfy the 'effective communicator' ideal in the workplace. 'Effective' is subject to changing definitions relative to factors such as the organization's desired corporate image, power and rapport status between interactants, the mode of interaction and the linguistic and cultural capital of clients, bosses and coworkers on- and offshore. With multiple standards of effectiveness simultaneously operative, there is a need for accountants to develop a professional habitus that can flexibly accommodate to the shifting notions of communication in the field. This habitus, while often explicitly shaped through formal pedagogy in school and corporate training, is mostly formed through socialization over years of professional experience, enabling them to get a better feel for how to navigate front- and backstage communication.

As a practical contribution to curricular innovation, this study proposes that the current accounting curriculum allocate more space for the following notions of communication that appear to be, in fact, significant in the workplace but only marginally recognized in school: multilingualism, digital literacy and interpersonal communication.

First, it is important for teachers to make future accountants aware that English is not the only language of globalized accounting work. It plays 'superstar' functions but only manages to do so with the equally important 'sidekick', the mother tongues shared by accountants. Knowing this, students may be encouraged to actively develop their proficiency not only in the hyper-central language but also in the peripheral ones that may occasionally, especially in relational talk, take a more central position in the interaction. In addition to Philippine languages, world languages other than English and different World Englishes may also be deployed by other globalized workers. These linguistic possibilities should form part of the imagination of future accountants and the curriculum should somehow equip them with intercultural competence and linguistic resourcefulness to manage this part of the job more confidently.

Second, with recruitment practices and work communication becoming increasingly dependent on technology in and beyond the globalized accounting field (thanks to the now-normal work-from-home setup), it is vital that students are taught how to use the different communication technologies that link remote work environments. Beyond pragmatism, this knowledge is also ideologically important as the findings highlight the strong connection between digital communication and trust impressions among geographically dispersed team members. While overseas partners and clients are predisposed to take a position of low trust, a more intentional digital literacy curriculum for future accountants can help them enter the work domain with some awareness and strategic knowledge on how to perform competence, productivity and trustworthiness on the digital platform. Concretely, this means training students not only how to answer common job interview questions and written tests but how to participate in these hiring rituals virtually. Evolving digitized recruitment rituals, such as online tests and interviews are important platforms on which to perform their virtual competence. It is therefore necessary for them to practice using various written and spoken digital channels for communication and so discover for themselves the affordances and limitations of each tool and strategize to mobilize them purposively.

Finally, it will benefit students to practice engaging in small talk in English, as experienced globalized accountants have identified this relational conversation in the workplace as a site of linguistic insecurity. Through supervised instruction and practice on how to start and sustain a conversation in English, accounting students may 'bleed' less and feel more comfortable in future globalized work small talk scenarios. Practically, this involves in-class role playing as well as 'real-life' (i.e. outside school) practice, and reflecting on what worked and what did not work in these learning encounters. Such deliberate effort to cultivate social fluency in English may empower accountants to practice agency more actively on the front stage rather than escaping to the back stage when asked by a non-Filipino how they are doing.

While I make these practical suggestions, I reemphasize the point that aligning academic and professional knowledge and practice is not the ultimate solution to make accountants 'better' communicators. This aim for alignment needs to be viewed with the understanding that the differential priorities of higher education and professional practice mean that the academic habitus and professional habitus can only be partially aligned at best. Whereas the accounting workplace is primarily driven by business goals, higher education is preoccupied with the twofold agenda of academic and vocational goals. To expect higher education to fully prepare students to be 'effective communicators' at work is to lose sight of the other pedagogical goals that teachers simultaneously juggle in the classroom. This study has demonstrated that this inevitable tension between academic goals and vocational goals needs to inform expectations of alignment.

In addition, this research shows that the academic habitus, while oriented toward the workplace, in turn shapes the professional habitus. This is reflected in the gatekeeping practice of administering written tests that resemble university admission exams with essay-type items and questions testing knowledge of English grammar and spelling. Even before getting to this stage, graduates sit the licensure exam that includes similar language items. Finally, teaching strategies for mandatory corporate communication training also resemble practices in classroom instruction and assessments. These continuities suggest that the accounting profession is also shaped by practices in higher education, demonstrating the bidirectional relation between the two domains. Acknowledging this mutuality is an initial step toward balancing the view that tends to overemphasize the onus on higher education to produce graduates that match the workplace standards of 'effective communication'.

Overall, this research argues for the need to be critical of the deficit model that perpetuates negative stereotypes and overburdens higher education with an unattainable goal. As this study has shown, the deficit discourse is problematic as it not only pigeonholes individuals into social categories but also thrusts them into an endless chase after an ideal that is constantly shifting and thus beyond full realization (Park, 2011). This hidden effect is part of the reason why it is necessary to go beyond the competence view of communication.

7.4 Hidden Language Work and the Digital Stage: Implications for Sociolinguistics

In sociolinguistics, this research contributes in terms of method and theory. In terms of research methods, this study demonstrates three approaches that can potentially enrich critical sociolinguistic ethnography. First, this research shows that examining together the education and work domains of a field can help provide a wider understanding of how language practices and ideologies are (re)produced, (re)shaped and (re)appropriated across interrelated field sites. Future studies can contribute more by further exploring ideological (dis)connections across these domains. Second, this research exemplifies the use of corpus methods as a tool to analyze the discursive construction of communication in documents authored by social actors. Whereas corpus techniques are more typically employed in quantitative research, qualitative investigations may also benefit from the use of these tools to identify patterns of linguistic ideologies in texts. Third, examining related written and spoken discourses in the field (e.g. curricular documents and classroom interactions; job ads and recruitment rituals) provides insight into (dis)continuities in entextualized and enacted discourses of language and communication in meso (institutional) and micro (individual) levels.

In terms of theory, this research partially fills important gaps in sociolinguistics scholarship. First, it responds to the need 'to diversify [the] knowledge base and the academic voices producing that knowledge base' (Piller *et al.*, 2020: 503). Specifically, it amplifies Global South voices, which are minimally heard in ongoing conversations about power and resistance related to language regimes in the new economy. This is important because existing scholarship has mostly echoed views from Anglophone sites about neoliberal capital formation. While these previous studies provide a background understanding of dominant language ideologies, this research brings to the fore communication issues that are widely taken for granted in Global North perspectives. For instance, the findings highlight tensions between performing authority and solidarity, creating global and local identity, and being controlled and exercising agency primarily through language use and digital channels. Similar issues have been raised in critical analyses of the linguistic experience of global, transnational workers, such as flight attendants (Piller & Takahashi, 2013), temporary skilled migrant workers (Piller & Lising, 2014), overseas domestic laborers (Lorente, 2012, 2018) and call center workers (Boussebaa *et al.*, 2014; Salonga, 2010). Following these studies, this research expands the scope of investigation to include the knowledge process outsourcing industry, particularly the growing field of offshore accounting, where the Philippines is an emerging global leader (Inventor-Miranda, 2016; 'Top accounting outsourcing destination countries compared', 2019).

This study has demonstrated that, while typically imagined as silent back-office workers, globalized accountants are, in fact, active language workers and their number-centric work is significantly intertwined with multiple communication practices and ideologies. This view is hidden partly due to the digital staging of communicative performances at work, which creates virtual front- and backstage spaces that are visible only to interactants in the field. These digital interactive spaces are sites for the reproduction of language hierarchies that prevail in physical interaction sites, where English is positioned front and center as the undisputed global language of accounting, and Philippine languages take on a supporting role. Besides reifying language hierarchies, digital channels tend to sharpen the focus on accountants' ability to communicate and de-emphasize their technical skills. Communication technologies also represent sites of surveillance, where accountants' productivity is constantly scrutinized, and where they are also constructed into virtual auditors of their teammates' compliance with neoliberal standards of efficiency.

Second, the findings reported in this study extend research into the performativity of language, which has previously focused on physical staging or embodied performance of communication mostly through spoken discourse (Bauman, 2011; Goffman, 1990). The analyses of written discourse in the form of digitized texts, such as education documents from institutional websites, online job ads and emails, demonstrate that written communications represent powerful sites for the reproduction of language hierarchies and ideologies about privileged forms of communication. The affordances of technology can even further enlarge these already-entrenched ideologies through faster and wider dissemination and replication. These insights therefore suggest the need to account for how the increasing technologization of work communication reproduces but also transforms rules, creating new ways of playing the language game in globalized settings.

7.5 Demystifying Old Labels and New Rules: Future Directions

Finally, the implications of this study point to possible directions for future research. First, there is much potential in further investigating the digitization of communication practices at work. While I have initially examined how this process (re)shapes communication ideologies in globalized accounting, more in-depth analyses of language performance at work in other fields through different written and spoken digital channels can be a valuable contribution to sociolinguistic literature on performance. For instance, investigations may look into dominant discourses of work talk (both spoken and written), language regulation and identity formation of social actors communicating through video conferencing and instant messaging applications. Comparing digital communication practices and ideologies in business process outsourcing and knowledge process outsourcing may also provide a more nuanced understanding of the distinctive ways that social actors in these industries communicate, and how the differential nature of offshore work (e.g. voice versus nonvoice service, customer-facing versus back-office work) shape standards of 'good' global professional communication. With the COVID-19 pandemic heightening technological dependencies in school and work, studies could also explore if and how the rules of the digital language game have been modified to suit the now-normative virtual ways of teaching and working, and what (if any) new tensions and opportunities arise from these practices.

Second, this study has demonstrated how the use of sociolinguistic lenses, especially through a critical ethnography of the education and work domains, can challenge occupational stereotypes by uncovering ideologies hidden behind labels such as 'shy quants', 'good with numbers, not words' and 'poor communicators'. I argue that stereotypes like these function as a form of 'verbal hygiene' (Cameron, 2012), a device that regulates social actors' attitude toward and investment in their communication skills. By intensifying their linguistic insecurity, this label challenges accountants (with extra pressure from teachers and employers) to break the stereotype by actively subordinating themselves to academic and corporate language regimes and the project of 'endless self-development [through the] continuous improvement of [their] linguistic skills' (Park, 2011: 445). However, there is also the other possibility of embracing the stereotype and reconstructing it into something positive like a badge of authenticity – that not being good with words is a trademark of a 'real' accountant. This alternative response then diminishes the attraction of and desire to invest toward becoming the idealized accountant who is good with both numbers and words. Although reflecting agency, this reappropriation of a negative label into a positive one also has the effect of further reinforcing the stereotype that fuels the 'contemporary obsession with "communication skills" and "communication problems"' (Cameron, 2002: 67).

Recognizing the insidious effect of social stereotypes, this research calls for more critical reading of other stereotypes using the analytic lenses of neoliberalism and performance. This approach can potentially demystify other myths prevailing in the new economy that reduce individuals to social categories and differentially (dis)advantage their speech and writing simply on the basis of membership in gender, racioethnic and occupational groups. Investigations of this kind, I believe, can potentially yield insights into aspects of globalized work communication that are taken for granted and help make the global, transnational playing field less uneven.

References

Acharya, M. (2017) Want to migrate to Australia? 2017–18 Skilled Occupations List announced: Department of Immigration and Border Protection (DIBP) have released the Skilled Occupations List (SOL) – 2017–18 effective 1st July. See https://www.sbs.com.au/yourlanguage/hindi/en/article/2017/06/30/want-migrate-australia-2017-18-skilled-occupations-list-announced.

Airey, J. (2009) *Science, Language and Literacy. Case Studies of Learning in Swedish University Physics*. Uppsala: Acta Universitatis Upsaliensis. See http://publications.uu.se/theses/abstract.xsql?dbid=9547

Airey, J. (2011) The disciplinary literacy discussion matrix: A heuristic tool for initiating collaboration in higher education. *Across the Disciplines* 8 (3), 1–9. See https://wac.colostate.edu/docs/atd/clil/airey.cfm

Albrecht, W.S. and Sack, R.J. (2000) *Accounting Education: Charting the Course Through a Perilous Future* (Vol. 16). Lakewood Ranch, FL: American Accounting Association.

Almario, V.S. (2014) *Madalas itanong hinggil sa wikang pambansa [Frequently asked questions on the national language]*. Manila: Komisyon sa Wikang Filipino.

Ameen, E., Bruns, S.M. and Jackson, C. (2010) Communication skills and accounting: Do perceptions match reality. *The CPA Journal* 80 (7), 63–65.

Ameen, E., Jackson, C. and Malgwi, C. (2010) Student perceptions of oral communication requirements in the accounting profession. *Global Perspectives on Accounting Education* 7, 31–49.

Anderson, M.O. (2013) Building accounting students communication skills. *Management Accounting Quarterly* 14 (4), 32–43.

Andrews, D.J. and Koester, R.J. (1973) Communication difficulties as perceived by the accounting professionals and professors of accounting. *The Journal of Business Communication* 16 (2), 33–42.

Andrews, D.J. and Sigband, N.B. (1984) How effectively does the 'new' accountant communicate? Perceptions by practitioners and academics. *The Journal of Business Communication* 21 (2), 15–24.

Angouri, J. (2010) 'If we know about culture it will be easier to work with one another': Developing skills for handling corporate meetings with multinational participation. *Language and Intercultural Communication* 10 (3), 206–224. https://doi.org/10.1080/14708470903348549

Angouri, J. (2014) Multilingualism in the workplace: Language practices in multilingual contexts. *Multilingua: Journal of Cross-Cultural and Interlanguage Communication* 33 (1–2), 1–9. https://doi.org/10.1515/multi-2014-0001

Anthony, L. (2019) *AntConc (Version 3.5.8) [Computer Software]*. In Waseda University. See www.lauenceanthony.net/software.html

Apat, E.J.C., De Villa, J.P.D. and Ibarra, V.C. (2019) Evolution, implementation and effects of international accounting standards in the Philippines. *Malaysian E Commerce Journal* 3 (2), 6–11. https://doi.org/10.26480/mecj.02.2019.06.11

Aranya, N., Meir, E.I. and Bar-Ilan, A. (1978) An empirical examination of the stereotype accountant based on Holland's theory. *Journal of Occupational Psychology* 51 (2), 139–145. https://doi.org/10.1111/j.2044-8325.1978.tb00408.x

Bals, L., Orberg Jensen, P.D., Larsen, M.M. and Pedersen, T. (2013) Exploring layers of complexity in offshoring research and practice. In T. Pedersen, L. Bals, P.D.O. Jensen and M.M. Larsen (eds) *The Offshoring Challenge: Strategic Design and Innovation for Tomorrow's Organization* (pp. 1–20). London: Springer.

Bauman, R. (1992) Performance. In R. Bauman (ed.) *Folklore, Cultural Performance, and Popular Entertainment* (pp. 41–49). Oxford: Oxford University Press.

Bauman, R. (2011) Commentary: Foundations in performance. *Journal of Sociolinguistics* 15 (5), 707–720. https://doi.org/10.1111/j.1467-9841.2011.00510.x

Bautista, M.L.S. (1982) Yaya English. *Philippine Studies* 30 (3), 377–394. See www.jstor.org/stable/42632617

Bautista, M.L.S. (1996) Notes on three sub-varieties of Philippine English. In M.L.S. Bautista (ed.) *Readings in Philippine Sociolinguistics* (pp. 93–101). Manila: De La Salle University.

Bautista, M.L.S. (1999) An analysis of the functions of Tagalog-English code switching: Data from one case. In M.L.S. Bautista and G.O. Tan (eds) *The Filipino Bilingual: A Multidisciplinary Perspective (Festschrift in Honor of Emy M. Pascasio)* (pp. 19–31). Manila: Linguistic Society of the Philippines.

Bautista, M.L.S. (2000) *Defining Standard Philippine English.* Manila: De La Salle University Press.

Bautista, M.L.S. (2004) Tagalog-english code switching as a mode of discourse. *Asia Pacific Education Review* 5 (2), 226–233. https://doi.org/10.1007/BF03024960

Bautista, M.L.S. (2008) Who's afraid of Philippine English? (Part 2). *Manila Bulletin*, 15 June.

Bernard, L. (2014) Accountant glut prompts skilled-migrant list rethink. *The Australian*, 29 January, p. 27. See https://www.theaustralian.com.au/search-results?q=Accountant+glut+prompts+skilled-migrant+list+rethink

Bernardo, A.S. (2017) Philippine English in the ESL classroom: A much closer look. *Philippine ESL Journal* 19 (2), 117–144.

Bernardo, A.S. (2022) Teaching (in) Philippine English. In A.M. Borlongan (ed.) *Philippine English: Development, Structure, and Sociology of English in the Philippines* (pp. 283–296). New York, NY: Routledge.

Bernardo, A.S. and Madrunio, M.R. (2015) A framework for designing a Philippine-English-based pedagogic model for teaching English grammar. *Asian Journal of English Language Studies* 3, 42–71.

Bhatia, V.K. (2008) Genre analysis, ESP and professional practice. *English for Specific Purposes* 27 (2), 161–174. https://doi.org/10.1016/j.esp.2007.07.005

Bhatia, V.K. (2010) Interdiscursivity in professional communication. *Discourse & Communication* 4 (1), 32–50. https://doi.org/10.1177/1750481309351208

Birrell, B. and Healy, E. (2008) How are skilled migrants doing? *People and Place* 16 (1), 1–20.

Blackmore, J., Gribble, C. and Rahimi, M. (2017) International education, the formation of capital and graduate employment: Chinese accounting graduates' experiences of the Australian labour market. *Critical Studies in Education* 58 (1), 69–88. https://doi.org/10.1080/17508487.2015.1117505

BOA Admin. (2015) *B.S. Accountancy Curriculum Revisions Forthcoming.* See https://boa.com.ph/2015/07/b-s-accountancy-curriculum-revisions-forthcoming/

Bourdieu, P. (1990) *The Logic of Practice* (trans. R. Nice). Stanford, CA: Stanford University Press.

Bourdieu, P. and Thompson, J.B. (eds) (1992) *Language and Symbolic Power* (trans. G. Raymond and M. Adamson). Cambridge: Polity.

Boussebaa, M., Sinha, S. and Gabriel, Y. (2014) Englishization in offshore call centers: A postcolonial perspective. *Journal of International Business Studies* 45 (9), 1152–1169. https://doi.org/10.1057/jibs.2014.25

Boyle, D.M., Mahoney, D.P., Carpenter, B.W. and Grambo, R.J. (2014) The importance of communication skills at different career levels. *The CPA Journal* 84 (8), 40–45.

Bruthiaux, P. (1996) *The Discourse of Classified Advertising: Exploring the Nature of Linguistic Simplicity*. Oxford: Oxford University Press.

Burns, A. and Moore, S. (2007) Conversation analysis and the accounting classroom: Exploring implications for LSP teaching. In H. Bowles and P. Seedhouse (eds) *Conversation Analysis and Language for Specific Purposes* (pp. 183–215). Bern: Peter Lang. http://hdl.handle.net/1959.14/34664

Butler, J. (1997) *Excitable Speech: A Politics of the Performative*. New York, NY: Routledge.

Cain, S. (2012) *Quiet: The Power of Introverts in a World That Can't Stop Talking*. New York, NY: Random House.

Cameron, D. (2000a) *Good to Talk: Living and Working in a Communication Culture*. London: Sage.

Cameron, D. (2000b) Styling the worker: Gender and the commodification of language in the globalized service economy. *Journal of Sociolinguistics* 4 (3), 323–347. https://doi.org/10.1111/1467-9481.00119

Cameron, D. (2002) Globalization and the teaching of 'communication skills'. In D. Block and D. Cameron (eds) *Globalization and Language Teaching* (pp. 67–82). New York, NY: Routledge.

Cameron, D. (2012) *Verbal Hygiene: The Politics of Language*. New York, NY: Routledge.

Canagarajah, S. (2000) Negotiating ideologies through English: Strategies from the periphery. In T. Ricento (ed.) *Ideology, Politics and Language Policies* (pp. 121–132). Amsterdam: John Benjamins Publishing Company.

Carey, J.L. (1965) *The CPA Plans for the Future*. New York, NY: American Institute of Certified Public Accountants.

Christensen, D.S. and Rees, D. (2002) An analysis of the business communication skills needed by entry-level accountants. *Mountain Plain Journal of Management and Economics* 3 (1), 62–75.

Claudio, L. (2014) CHED is not targeting Filipino language instruction. See https://www.rappler.com/thought-leaders/61039-ched-filipino-language (accessed 4 June 2019).

Commission on Higher Education [CHED] (n.d.) The transition in higher education. See https://chedk12.wordpress.com/transition-in-higher-education/

Commission on Higher Education [CHED] (2013) *General education curriculum: Holistic understandings, intellectual and civic competencies* (Memorandum Order No. 20, series 2013). See https://ched.gov.ph/wp-content/uploads/2017/10/CMO-No.20-s2013.pdf

Costley, T. (2014) What's in a name? Power, space, and the negotiation of identities. In Y.L. Cheung, S.B. Said and K. Park (eds) *Advances and Current Trends in Language Teacher Identity Research* (pp. 74–85). London: Taylor and Francis.

Coulmas, F. (2013) *Writing and Society*. Cambridge: Cambridge University Press.

Dadas, C. (2018) Interview practices as accessibility: The academic job market. *Composition Forum* 39. http://compositionforum.com/issue/39/interview-practices.php

Darang, J.A.Z., Diwa, J.P.G., Domasig, D.P.S., Lubong, K.M.D., Tenedero, P.P.P. and Tuazon Jr., A.M. (2015) Are future Philippine business professionals afraid to speak? A communication apprehension profile of accountancy and tourism majors. *Asian Journal of English Language Studies* 3, 72–89.

de Swaan, A. (2001) *Words of the World: The Global Language System*. Cambridge: Polity Press.

Del Percio, A. (2018) Turning language and communication into productive resources: Language policy and planning and multinational corporations. In J.W. Tollefson and M. Pérez-Milans (eds) *The Oxford Handbook of Language Policy and Planning* (pp. 1–18). Oxford: Oxford University Press.

DepEd Resources (2017) Main features of the enhanced K to 12 curriculum. See https://www.depedresources.com/download-k-12-curriculum-guides/

Detzen, D. and Loehlein, L. (2018) Language at work in the Big Four: Global aspirations and local segmentation. *Accounting, Auditing & Accountability* 31 (7), 2031–2054. https://doi.org/10.1108/AAAJ-06-2017-2968

Dlaske, K. (2016) Shaping subjects of globalisation: At the intersection of voluntourism and the new economy. *Multilingua: Journal of Cross-Cultural and Interlanguage Communication* 35 (4), 415–440. https://doi.org/10.1515/multi-2015-0002

Dlaske, K., Barakos, E., Motobayashi, K. and Mclaughlin, M. (2016) Languaging the worker: Globalized governmentalities in/of language in peripheral spaces. *Multilingua: Journal of Cross-Cultural and Interlanguage Communication* 35 (4), 345–359. https://doi.org/10.1515/multi-2015-0009

Dong, J. and Blommaert, J. (2009) Space, scale and accents: Constructing migrant identity in Beijing. *Multilingua* 28, 1–24. https://doi.org/10.1515/mult.2009.001

Duchêne, A. (2008) *Ideologies Across Nations: The Construction of Linguistic Minorities at the United Nations*. Berlin: Mouton de Gruyter.

Duchêne, A., Moyer, M. and Roberts, C. (eds) (2013) *Language, Migration and Social Inequalities: A Critical Sociolinguistic Perspective on Institutions and Work*. Bristol: Multilingual Matters.

Dumanig, F.P., David, M.K. and Symaco, L. (2012) Competing roles of the national language and English in Malaysia and the Philippines: Planning, policy and use. *Journal of International and Comparative Education* 1 (2), 104–115. https://doi.org/10.14425/00.45.77

Dunn, C.D. (2013) Speaking politely, kindly, and beautifully: Ideologies of politeness in Japanese business etiquette training. *Multilingua* 32 (2), 225–245. https://doi.org/10.1515/multi-2013-0011

Dyball, M.C., Poullaos, C. and Chua, W.F. (2007) Accounting and empire: Professionalization-as-resistance: The case of Philippines. *Critical Perspectives on Accounting* 18 (4), 415–449. https://doi.org/10.1016/j.cpa.2006.01.008

Ellis, E.M., Gogolin, I. and Clyne, M. (2010) The Janus face of monolingualism: A comparison of German and Australian language education policies. *Current Issues in Language Planning* 11 (4), 439–460. https://doi.org/10.1080/14664208.2010.550544

Evans, L. (2018) Language, translation and accounting: Towards a critical research agenda. *Accounting, Auditing & Accountability* 31 (7), 1844–1873. https://doi.org/10.1108/AAAJ-08-2017-3055

Evans, L. and Kamla, R. (2018) Language and translation in accounting: A scandal of silence and displacement? *Accounting, Auditing & Accountability* 31 (7), 1834–1843. https://doi.org/10.1108/AAAJ-09-2018-020

Fairclough, N. (2003) *Analysing Discourse: Textual Analysis for Social Research*. London: Routledge.

Fairclough, N. (2010) *Critical Discourse Analysis: The Critical Study of Language* (2nd edn). Harlow: Longman.

Fletcher, J. (2017) Rapport management. In B. Vine (ed.) *The Routledge Handbook of Language in the Workplace* (pp. 77–88). London: Routledge.

Flores, N. and Rosa, J. (2015) Undoing appropriateness: Raciolinguistic ideologies and language diversity in education. *Harvard Educational Review* 85 (2), 149–171.

García, O. (2014) Countering the dual: Transglossia, dynamic bilingualism and translanguaging in education. In R. Rubdy and L. Alsagoff (eds) *The Global-Local Interface and Hybridity: Exploring Language and Identity* (pp. 100–118). Bristol: Multilingual Matters.

Gardner, C.T., Milne, M.J., Stringer, C.P. and Whiting, R.H. (2005) Oral and written communication apprehension in accounting students: Curriculum impacts and impacts on academic performance. *Accounting Education* 14 (3), 313–336. https://doi.org/10.1080/06939280500077269

Geronimo, J.Y. (2014) No Filipino subjects in college? 'Tanggol Wika' opposes CHED memo. See https://www.rappler.com/nation/61234-tanggol-wika-general-education-college (accessed 4 June 2019).

Gershon, I. (2019) Hailing the US job-seeker: Origins and neoliberal uses of job applications. *Culture, Theory and Critique* 60 (1), 84–97. https://doi.org/10.1080/14735784.2018.1548299

Gist-Mackey, A.N. (2018) (Dis)embodied job search communication training: Comparative critical ethnographic analysis of materiality and discourse during the unequal search for work. *Organization Studies* 39 (9), 1251–1275. https://doi.org/10.1177/0170840617736936

Go, M.A. and Gustilo, L. (2013) Tagalog or Taglish: The lingua franca of Filipino urban factory workers. *Philippine ESL Journal* 10, 57–87.

Goffman, E. (1974) *Stigma: Notes on the Management of Spoiled Identity*. New York, NY: J. Aronson.

Goffman, E. (1981) *Forms of Talk*. Philadelphia, PA: University of Pennsylvania Press.

Goffman, E. (1990) *The Presentation of Self in Everyday Life*. London: Penguin Psychology.

Granleese, J. and Barrett, T.F. (1990) The social and personality characteristics of the Irish chartered accountant. *Personality and Individual Differences* 11 (9), 957–964.

Gray, F.E. (2010) Specific oral communication skills desired in new accountancy graduates. *Business Communication Quarterly* 73 (1), 40–67. https://doi.org/10.1177/1080569909356350

Gray, F.E. and Murray, N. (2011) 'A distinguishing factor': Oral communication skills in new accountancy graduates. *Accounting Education* 20 (3), 275–294. https://doi.org/10.1080/09639284.2011.560763

Grossi, V. (2012) Ways of working and ways of speaking: A linguistic ethnography of migrant IT professionals in Australian workplaces. Doctoral dissertation, Macquarie University, Sydney, Australia.

Gu, M. (2014) From opposition to transcendence: The language practices and ideologies of students in a multilingual university. *International Journal of Bilingual Education and Bilingualism* 17 (3), 310–329. https://doi.org/10.1080/13670050.2013.766148

Handford, M. (2015) Corpus analysis. In Z. Hua (ed.) *Research Methods in Intercultural Communication: A Practical Guide* (pp. 311–326). Hoboken, NJ: John Wiley & Sons.

Hassall, T., Joyce, J., Ottewill, R., Arquero, J. and Donoso, J. (2000) Communication apprehension in UK and Spanish business and accounting students. *Education Training* 42 (2), 93–100. https://doi.org/10.1108/EUM0000000005351

Heller, M. and Duchêne, A. (2012) Pride and profit: Changing discourses of language, capital and nation-state. In A. Duchêne and M. Heller (eds) *Language in Late Capitalism: Pride and Profit* (pp. 1–21). New York, NY: Routledge.

Henderson, K.I. (2017) Teacher language ideologies mediating classroom-level language policy in the implementation of dual language bilingual education. *Linguistics and Education* 42, 21–33. https://doi.org/10.1016/j.linged.2017.08.003

Holborow, M. (2018) Language skills as human capital? Challenging the neoliberal frame. *Language and Intercultural Communication* 18 (5), 520–532. https://doi.org/10.1080/14708477.2018.1501846

Holmes, J. (2007) Monitoring organisational boundaries: Diverse discourse strategies used in gatekeeping. *Journal of Pragmatics* 39 (11), 1993–2016. https://doi.org/10.1016/j.pragma.2007.07.009

Iedema, R. and Wodak, R. (1999) Introduction: Organizational discourses and practices. *Discourse & Society* 10 (1), 5–19. https://doi.org/10.1177/0957926599010001001

Inventor-Miranda, W.C. (2008) The financial executive wild ride for outsourcing. *BusinessWorld*, 4 March. See https://global.factiva.com/ha/default.aspx#./!?&_suid=1569285257123077696869714664 34

Inventor-Miranda, W.C. (2016) Update on finance and accounting outsourcing. *BusinessMirror*, 28 July. See https://global.factiva.com/ha/default.aspx#./!?&_suid=156928553226006728323729914798

Inventor-Miranda, W.C. (2017) F and A outsourcing - Not just an option but a necessity. *Business Mirror*, 12 October. See https://businessmirror.com.ph/2017/10/12/fa-outsourcing-not-just-an-option-but-a-necessity/

Jeacle, I. (2008) Beyond the boring grey: The construction of the colourful accountant. *Critical Perspectives on Accounting* 19 (8), 1296–1320. https://doi.org/10.1016/j.cpa.2007.02.008

Jenkins, J. (2017) Mobility and English language policies and practices in higher education. In S. Canagarajah (ed.) *The Routledge Handbook of Migration and Language* (pp. 502–518). New York, NY: Routledge.

Jiang, Y.G. (2014) *Liberal Arts Education in a Changing Society: A New Perspective on Chinese Higher Education*. Leiden: Brill. https://doi.org/10.1163/9789004282315_002

Johnson, R. (2014) Accounting practitioners reflect on faculty impact: Bridging the gap between theory and practice. *American Journal of Business Education* 7 (2), 109–114. https://doi.org/10.19030/ajbe.v7i2.8469

Jones, C.G. (2011) Written and computer-mediated accounting communication skills. *Business Communication Quarterly* 74 (3), 247–271. https://doi.org/10.1177/1080569911413808

Jørgensen, J.N. (2008) Polylingual languaging around and among children and adolescents. *International Journal of Multilingualism* 5 (3), 161–176.

Kachru, B.B. (ed.) (1992) *The Other Tongue: English Across Cultures* (2nd edn). Chicago, IL: University of Illinois.

Kamla, R. and Komori, N. (2018) Diagnosing the translation gap: The politics of translation and the hidden contradiction in interdisciplinary accounting research. *Accounting, Auditing & Accountability* 31 (7), 1874–1903. https://doi.org/10.1108/AAAJ-08-2017-3067

Kavanagh, M.H. and Drennan, L. (2008) What skills and attributes does an accounting graduate need? Evidence from student perceptions and employer expectations. *Accounting & Finance* 48 (2), 279–300. https://doi.org/10.1111/j.1467-629X.2007.00245.x

Kettunen, J. (2017) Interlingual translation of the International Financial Reporting Standards as institutional work. *Accounting, Organizations and Society* 56, 38–54. https://doi.org/10.1016/j.aos.2016.10.001

King, R., Blayney, P. and Sweller, J. (2021) How language background impacts learners studying International Financial Reporting Standards: A cognitive load theory perspective. *Accounting Education* 30 (5), 439–450. https://doi.org/10.1080/09639284.2021.1930562

Kirilova, M. and Angouri, J. (2017) Communication practices and policies in workplace mobility. In S. Canagarajah (ed.) *The Routledge Handbook of Migration and Language* (pp. 540–557). New York, NY: Routledge.

Kleibert, J.M. (2014) Strategic coupling in 'next wave cities': Local institutional actors and the offshore service sector in the Philippines. *Singapore Journal of Tropical Geography* 35 (2), 245–260. https://doi.org/10.1111/sjtg.12044

Kleibert, J.M. (2015) Expanding global production networks: The emergence, evolution and the developmental impact of the offshore service sector in the Philippines. Doctoral Dissertation, University of Amsterdam, The Netherlands. See https://dare.uva.nl/search?identifier=c33c8769-2f5a-448e-aca7-3b5448926aba

Kuteeva, M. and Airey, J. (2014) Disciplinary differences in the use of English in higher education: Reflections on recent language policy developments. *Higher Education* 67 (5), 533–549. https://doi.org/10.1007/s10734-013-9660-6

Lea, M.R. and Street, B.V. (1998) Student writing in higher education: An academic literacies approach. *Studies in Higher Education* 23 (2), 157–172. https://doi.org/10.1080/03075079812331380364

Leung, C. and Valdés, G. (2019) Translanguaging and the transdisciplinary framework for language teaching and learning in a multilingual world. *Modern Language Journal* 103 (2), 348–370. https://doi.org/10.1111/modl.12568

Lin, P., Grace, D., Krishnan, S. and Gilsdorf, J. (2010) Failure to communicate: Why accounting students don't measure up to professionals' expectations. *The CPA Journal* 80 (1), 63.
Lipovsky, C. (2006) Candidates' negotiation of their expertise in job interviews. *Journal of Pragmatics* 38 (8), 1147–1174. https://doi.org/10.1016/j.pragma.2005.05.00
Lipovsky, C. (2008) Constructing affiliation and solidarity in job interviews. *Discourse & Communication* 2 (4), 411–432. https://doi.org/10.1177/1750481308095938
Lippi-Green, R. (2012) *English with an Accent: Language, Ideology and Discrimination in the United States* (2nd edn). New York, NY: Routledge.
Lising, L., Peters, P. and Smith, A. (2020) Code-switching in online academic discourse Resources for Philippine English. *English World-Wide* 41 (2), 131–161. https://doi.org/10.1075/eww.00044.lis
Littleton, A. and Zimmerman, V.K. (1962) *Accounting Theory, Continuity and Change.* Englewood Cliffs, NJ: Prentice-Hall.
Lockwood, J. (2012) Are we getting the right people for the job? A study of English language recruitment assessment practices in the business processing outsourcing sector: India and the Philippines. *Journal of Business Communication* 49 (2), 107–127. https://doi.org/10.1177/0021943612436975
Lorente, B.P. (2012) The making of "workers of the world": Language and the labor brokerage state. In A. Duchêne and M. Heller (eds) *Language in Late Capitalism: Pride and Profit* (pp. 183–206). New York, NY: Routledge.
Lorente, B.P. (2017). Language-in-education policies and mobile citizens. In S. Canagarajah (ed.) *The Routledge Handbook of Migration and Language* (pp. 486–501). New York, NY: Routledge.
Lorente, B.P. (2018). *Scripts of Servitude: Language, Labor Migration and Transnational Domestic Work.* Bristol: Multilingual Matters.
Louhiala-Salminen, L. and Kankaanranta, A. (2011) Professional communication in a global business context: The notion of global communicative competence. *IEEE Transactions on Professional Communication* 54 (3), 244–262. https://doi.org/10.1109/TPC.2011.2161844
Lüdi, G. (2017) Identity in the workplace in a context of increasing multilingualism. In B. Vine (ed.) *The Routledge Handbook of Language in the Workplace* (pp. 348–360). New York, NY: Routledge.
Miller, T.C. and Stone, D.N. (2009) Public speaking apprehension, motivation, and affect among accounting majors: A proof-of-concept intervention. *Issues in Accounting Education* 24 (3), 265–298. https://doi.org/10.2308/iace.2009.24.3.265
Moore, R. (2014) Capital. In M. Grenfell (ed.) *Pierre Bourdieu: Key Concepts* (pp. 101–117). Stocksfield: Acumen Publishing.
Morales, J. and Lambert, C. (2013) Dirty work and the construction of identity. An ethnographic study of management accounting practices. *Accounting, Organizations and Society* 38 (3), 228–244. https://doi.org/10.1016/j.aos.2013.04.001
Mounce, P.H., Mauldin, D.S. and Braun, R.L. (2004) The importance of relevant practical experience among accounting faculty: An empirical analysis of students' perceptions. *Issues in Accounting Education* 19 (4), 399–411. https://doi.org/10.2308/iace.2004.19.4.399
Natter, E. (2018) Why is accounting often referred to as the language of business? *Chron.com.* See https://smallbusiness.chron.com/can-accounting-make-difference-company-23530.html
Nellermoe, D.A., Weirich, T.R. and Reinstein, A. (1999) Using practitioners' viewpoints to improve accounting students communication skills. *Business Communication Quarterly* 62 (2), 41–56. https://doi.org/10.1177/108056999906200205
O'Keeffe, A., McCarthy, M. and Carter, R. (2007) *From Corpus to Classroom: Language Use and Language Teaching.* Cambridge: Cambridge University Press.
Osborne, D. (2018) "Ay, nosebleed!": Negotiating the place of English in contemporary Philippine linguistic life. *Language and Communication* 58, 118–133. https://doi.org/10.1016/j.langcom.2017.08.001

Parba, J. (2018) Teachers' shifting language ideologies and teaching practices in Philippine mother tongue classrooms. *Linguistics and Education* 47, 27–35. https://doi.org/10.1016/j.linged.2018.07.005

Park, J.S.-Y. (2011) The promise of English: Linguistic capital and the neoliberal worker in the South Korean job market. *International Journal of Bilingual Education and Bilingualism* 14 (4), 443–455. https://doi.org/10.1080/13670050.2011.573067

Pennycook, A. (2000a) English, politics, ideology: From colonial celebration to postcolonial performativity. In T. Ricento (ed.) *Ideology, Politics and Language Policies* (pp. 107–120). Amsterdam: John Benjamins Publishing Company.

Pennycook, A. (2000b) Language, ideology and hindsight: Lessons from colonial language policies. In T. Ricento (ed.) *Ideology, Politics and Language Policies* (pp. 49–66). Amsterdam: John Benjamins Publishing Company.

Pennycook, A. (2004) Performativity and language studies. *Critical Inquiry in Language Studies* 1 (1), 1–19. https://doi.org/10.1207/s15427595cils0101_1

Pennycook, A. (2007) *Global Englishes and Transcultural Flows*. New York, NY: Routledge.

Piller, I. (2010) Academic capitalism and the spread of English. *Language on the Move*, 11 July. See https://www.languageonthemove.com/academic-capitalism-and-the-spread-of-english/

Piller, I. (2016) *Linguistic Diversity and Social Justice: An Introduction to Applied Sociolinguistics*. Oxford: Oxford University Press.

Piller, I. (2017a) *Intercultural Communication: A Critical Introduction* (2nd edn). Edinburgh: Edinburgh University Press.

Piller, I. (2017b) Literacy – The power code. *Langauge on the Move*, 7 August. See http://www.languageonthemove.com/literacy-the-power-code/

Piller, I. (2019) On the conditions of authority in academic publics. *Journal of Sociolinguistics* 23 (5), 521–528. https://doi.org/10.1111/josl.12393

Piller, I. and Cho, J. (2013) Neoliberalism as language policy. *Language in Society* 42 (1), 23–44. https://doi.org/10.1111/josl.12185

Piller, I. and Takahashi, K. (2013) Language work aboard the low-cost airline. In A. Duchêne, M. Moyer and C. Roberts (eds) *Language, Migration and Social Inequalities: A Critical Sociolinguistic Perspective on Institutions and Work* (pp. 95–117). Bristol: Multilingual Matters.

Piller, I. and Lising, L. (2014) Language, employment, and settlement: Temporary meat workers in Australia. *Multilingua* 33 (1–2), 35–59. https://doi.org/10.1515/multi-2014-0003

Piller, I., Zhang, J. and Li, J. (2020) Linguistic diversity in a time of crisis: Language challenges of the COVID-19 pandemic. *Multilingua* 39 (5), 503–515. https://doi.org/10.1515/multi-2020-0136

Power, M. (1994) *The Audit Explosion*. London: Demos.

Rafaeli, A. and Oliver, A.L. (1998) Employment ads: A configurational research agenda. *Journal of Management Inquiry* 7 (4), 342–358. https://doi.org/10.1177/105649269874009

Rebele, J.E. (1985) An examination of accounting students' perceptions of the importance of communication skills in public accounting. *Issues in Accounting Education* 3 (1), 41–50.

Reves, W.F. (1946) The human side of auditing. *The Accounting Review* 21 (1), 82–84.

Reyes, A. (2017) Ontology of fake: Discerning the Philippine elite. *Signs and Society* 5 (1), 100–127. https://doi.org/10.1086/690067

Ricento, T. (2018) Globalization, language policy, and the role of English. In J.W. Tollefson and M. Pérez-Milans (eds) *The Oxford Handbook of Language Policy and Planning* (pp. 1–16). Oxford: Oxford University Press.

Roberts, C. (2013) The gatekeeping of Babel: Job interviews and the linguistic penalty. In A. Duchêne, M. Moyer and C. Roberts (eds) *Language, Migration and Social Inequalities: A Critical Sociolinguistic Perspective on Institutions and Work* (pp. 81–94). Bristol: Multilingual Matters.

Rodao, F. (1997) Spanish language in the Philippines: 1900-1940. *Philippine Studies* 45 (1), 94–107.

Roy, R.H. and MacNeill, J.H. (1970) Written and spoken English for the accountant. *The ABCA Journal of Business Communication* 7 (4), 39–44.

Salonga, A.O. (2010) Language and situated agency: An exploration of the dominant linguistic and communication practices in the Philippine offshore call centers. Doctoral Dissertation, National University of Singapore.

Scott, J.C. (1985) *Weapons of the Weak: Everyday Forms of Peasant Resistance.* New Haven, CT: Yale University Press.

Shohamy, E. (2006) *Language Policy: Hidden Agendas and New Approaches.* New York, NY: Routledge.

Shome, R. (2006) Thinking through the diaspora: Call centers, India, and a new politics of hybridity. *International Journal of Cultural Studies* 9 (1), 105–124. https://doi.org/10.1177/1367877906061167

Shore, C. and Wright, S. (2000) Coercive accountability: The rise of audit culture in higher education. In M. Strathern (ed.) *Audit Cultures* (pp. 57–89). New York, NY: Routledge.

Sibayan, B.P. and Gonzalez, A. (1996) Post-imperial English in the Philippines. In J.A. Fishman, A.W. Conrad and A. Rubal-Lopez (eds) *Post-Imperial English: Status Change in Former British and American Colonies, 1940–1990* (pp. 139–172). New York, NY: Mouton de Gruyter.

Simons, K., Higgins, M. and Lowe, D. (1995) A profile of communication apprehension in accounting majors: Implications for teaching and curriculum revision. *Journal of Accounting Education* 13 (2), 159–176. https://doi.org/10.1016/0748-5751(95)00001-3

Siu, N., Dickinson, J. and Lee, B. (2000) Ethical evaluations of business activities and personal religiousness. *Teaching Business Ethics* 4 (3), 239–256. https://doi.org/10.1023/A:1009886711972

Smith, B., Maguire, W. and Han, H.H. (2018) Generic skills in accounting: Perspectives of Chinese postgraduate students. *Accounting & Finance* 58 (2), 535–559. https://doi.org/10.1111/acfi.12219

Sodhi, M.S. and Son, B.-G. (2010) Content analysis of OR job advertisements to infer required skills. *Journal of the Operational Research Society* 61 (9), 1315–1327. https://doi.org/10.1057/jors.2009.80

Spence, C. and Carter, C. (2014) An exploration of the professional habitus in the Big 4 accounting firms. *Work, Employment and Society* 28 (6), 946–962. https://doi.org/10.1177/0950017013510762

Stone, G. and Lightbody, M. (2012) The nature and significance of listening skills in accounting practice. *Accounting Education* 21 (4), 363–384. https://doi.org/10.1080/09639284.2011.617062

Strathern, M. (ed.) (2000) *Audit Cultures: Anthropological Studies in Accountability, Ethics and the Academy.* New York, NY: Routledge.

Suttipun, M. (2012) Readiness of accounting students in the ASEAN Economic Community: An empirical study from Thailand. Mae Fah Luang University International Conference, Bangkok, Thailand.

Swain, M.R. and Olsen, K.J. (2012) From student to accounting professional: A longitudinal study of the filtering process. *Issues in Accounting Education* 27 (1), 17–52. https://doi.org/10.2308/iace-50076

Tamtomo, K. (2018) Institution and market: Orders of multiple languages in Indonesian vocational education. *Multilingua: Journal of Cross-Cultural and Interlanguage Communication* 37 (5), 429–454. https://doi.org/10.1515/multi-2017-0041

Tenedero, P.P.P. (2017) Accounting students' perspective of work-relevant communication skills: Evidence from a Philippine university. *Journal on English Language Teaching* 7 (1), 30–42.

Tenedero, P.P.P. and Vizconde, C.J. (2015) University English and audit firms in the Philippines: Meeting needs, merging deeds. *Business and Professional Communication Quarterly* 78 (4), 428–453. https://doi.org/10.1177/2329490615596154

Tenedero, P.P.P. and Orias, B.L. (2016) English that counts: Designing a purposive communication course for future accountants. *English for Specific Purposes World* 17 (50), 1–22.

Tenedero, P.P.P., Alcantara, A.A.S., Dagui, A.C.L., Lim, C.R., Palomeno, T.R.M. and Rosario, B.M.S. (2018) Oral communication in accounting practice: Perspectives from the Philippines. *Journal on English Language Teaching* 8 (2), 1–13. https://doi.org/10.26634/jelt.8.2.14585

Thomson, P. (2014) Field. In M. Grenfell (ed.) *Pierre Bourdieu: Key Concepts* (pp. 67–81). Stocksfield: Acumen Publishing.

Tolentino-Baysa, G. (2015) Revisions in the CPA licensure examination. *Business Mirror*, 5 November. See https://businessmirror.com.ph/2015/11/02/revisions-in-the-cpa-licensure-examination/

Top accounting outsourcing destination countries compared (2019) See https://theoutsourcedaccountant.com/blog/outsourcing-countries-comparison/

Torsh, H. (2012) Is bilingualism impolite? *Language on the Move*, 15 May. See https://www.languageonthemove.com/is-bilingualism-impolite/

Tupas, R. (2004) The politics of Philippine English: Neocolonialism, global politics, and the problem of postcolonialism. *World Englishes* 23 (1), 47–58. https://doi.org/10.1111/j.1467-971X.2004.00334.x

Tupas, R. and Tabiola, H. (2017) Language policy and development aid: A critical analysis of an ELT project. *Current Issues in Language Planning* 18 (4), 407–421. https://doi.org/10.1080/14664208.2017.1351329

Urciuoli, B. (2008) Skills and selves in the new workplace. *American Ethnologist* 35 (2), 211–228. https://doi.org/10.1111/j.1548-1425.2008.00031.x

Urciuoli, B. (2010) Entextualizing diversity: Semiotic incoherence in institutional discourse. *Language and Communication* 30 (1), 48–57. https://doi.org/10.1016/j.langcom.2009.10.005

Urciuoli, B. (2014) The semiotic production of the good student: A Peircean look at the commodification of liberal arts education. *Signs and Society* 2 (1), 56–83. https://doi.org/10.1086/675537

Urciuoli, B. and LaDousa, C. (2013) Language management/labor. *Annual Review of Anthropology* 42 (1), 175–190. https://doi.org/10.1146/annurev-anthro-092412-155524

Urla, J. (2012) Total quality language revival. In A. Duchêne and M. Heller (eds) *Language in Late Capitalism: Pride and Profit* (pp. 73–92). New York, NY: Routledge.

Urla, J. (2019) Governmentality and language. *Annual Review of Anthropology* 48, 261–278. https://doi.org/10.1146/annurev-anthro-102317-050258

Valanju, S. (2005). Site unseen? *Financial Management* July/August, 16–20.

VanZante, N.R. and Person, S. (1994) The new CPA examination. *The CPA Journal* 64 (4), 42–47.

Vizconde, C.J. (2011) When language use doesn't see eye to eye: Language practices of teachers and students in a Philippine comprehensive university. *KEDI Journal of Educational Policy* 8 (1), 123–141. https://doi.org/10.22804/kjep.2011.8.1.006

Vizconde, C.J. (2017) Evolving the university language policy from the lens of the administrators: Language beliefs and practices of university administrators in the Philippines. *KEDI Journal of Educational Policy* 14 (2), 61–77. https://doi.org/10.22804/kjep.2017.14.2.004

VRL Knowledgebank (2006) News digest: Migrant accountants struggle to find work in Australia. *Intercultural Accounting*, 12 December. See https://global.factiva.com/ga/default.aspx

Watts, R.J. (2011) *Language Myths and the History of English*. Oxford: Oxford University Press.

Weaver, P. and Kulesza, M. (2014) Critical skills for new accounting hires: What's missing from traditional college education? *Academy of Business Research Journal* 4, 34–49.
Weller, S.A. (2017) Accounting for skill shortages? Migration and the Australian Labour Market. *Population, Space and Place* 23 (2). https://doi.org/10.1002/psp.1997
Williams, G. (2011) Development: Part 1. In J. Agnew and J. Duncan (eds) *The Wiley-Blackwell Companion to Human Geography* (pp. 559–574). Oxford: Wiley-Blackwell.
Williams, G., Meth, P. and Willis, K. (2014) *Geographies of Developing Areas: The Global South in a Changing World* (2nd edn). New York, NY: Routledge.
Zaid, O.A. and Abraham, A. (1994) Communication skills in accounting education: Perceptions of academics, employers and graduate accountants. *Accounting Education* 3 (3), 205–221. https://doi.org/10.1080/09639289400000020
Zarei, R., Esmaeeli, A. and Zarei, S. (2016) Studying the influential factors on ethics in accounting and auditing regarding personal dimensions. *International Business Management* 10 (7), 1141–1150.

Appendix: Profile of Participants

Table A1 Teachers in accounting schools

Pseudonym	Teaching experience	Course taught	Languages spoken
Ms Aurora	25 years	English language	English, Filipino, Visayan
Mr Basilio	15 years	Accounting	English, Filipino, Kinaray-a
Mr Carlo	15 years	Accounting	English, Filipino, Cebuano, Hiligaynon, Ilocano
Ms Diwata	21 years	Accounting	English, Filipino
Ms Edna	22 years	Filipino language	English, Filipino
Mr Fernando	20 years	Accounting	English, Filipino
Mr Gregorio	4 years	Accounting	English, Filipino
Ms Helena	13 years	Business	English, Filipino, Visayan

Table A2 Accounting students

Pseudonym	Grade/Year level	Languages spoken
Isko	Year 5	English, Filipino, Fukien, Mandarin
Jaya	Year 3	English, Filipino, Chinese
Kriselda	Grade 12	English, Filipino, Bicolano, Waray
Lorenzo	Grade 12	English, Filipino, Tagalog, Waray
Maria	Year 4	English, Filipino, Bicolano
Nico	Year 1	English, Filipino
Olivia	Year 5	English, Filipino / Tagalog, Chinese, Hokkien, Japanese, Mandarin
Paco	Year 1	English, Filipino, Arabic
Quinto	Year 1	English, Filipino

Table A3 Gatekeepers in accounting workplaces

Pseudonym	Role	Type of organization
Boss Tita	Company owner and director	Offshore virtual loans assistance, administrative services
Boss Urduja	Human resource associate director	Finance and accounting outsourcing
Boss Vangie	Company cofounder	Finance and accounting outsourcing
Boss Wendell	Company cofounder	Finance and accounting outsourcing

Table A4 Globalized accountants

Pseudonym	Onshore/Offshore practice	Accounting experience	Languages
Accountant Alma	Offshore	11–15	English, Filipino
Accountant Brando	Offshore	1–5 years	English, Filipino, Hiligaynon
Accountant Corina	Offshore	1–5 years	English, Tagalog
Accountant Divina	Offshore	1–5 years	English, Filipino
Accountant Eva	Offshore	Less than 1 year	English, Tagalog
Accountant Fatima	Offshore	1–5 years	English, Filipino
Accountant Gina	Offshore	Less than 1 year	English, Tagalog
Accountant Hilda	Offshore	1–5 years	English, Tagalog, Ilocano
Accountant Ida	Offshore	1–5 years	English, Taglish
Accountant Julia	Onshore	1–5 years	English, Filipino
Accountant Karla	Onshore	6–10 years	English, Tagalog
Accountant Lara	Onshore	6–10 years	English, Filipino
Accountant Myrna	Onshore	6–10 years	English, Tagalog
Accountant Nadia	Onshore	1–5 years	English, Tagalog
Accountant Orlando	Onshore	11–15 years	English, Filipino, Ilonggo, Visayan
Accountant Paloma	Onshore	Over 20 years	English, Filipino
Accountant Rosario	Onshore	1–5 years	English, Filipino, Pampango
Accountant Stella	Onshore	Over 20 years	Filipino, English, Ibanag

Index

For Product Safety Concerns and Information please contact our EU Authorised Representative:

Easy Access System Europe

Mustamäe tee 50

10621 Tallinn

Estonia

gpsr.requests@easproject.com

www.ingramcontent.com/pod-product-compliance
Ingram Content Group UK Ltd.
Pitfield, Milton Keynes, MK11 3LW, UK
UKHW021836150926
8656IPUK00003B/15

* 9 7 8 1 8 0 0 4 1 6 4 7 5 *